BASIC TRAINING

FOR PER$ONAL

MILITARY

FINANCE

BASIC TRAINING

FOR PER$ONAL

MILITARY

FINANCE

INVESTMENT STRATEGIES TO PUT
YOUR MILITARY PAY ON ACTIVE DUTY

MICHAEL STEPHEN HAMLIN

MILITARY MILLIONAIRES, LLC | LUFKIN, TX

Published by
Military Millionaires, LLC
Lufkin, TX

Publisher's Cataloging-in-Publication Data
Hamlin, Michael Stephen.

Basic training for personal military finance : investment strategies to put your military pay on active duty / Michael Stephen Hamlin. – Lufkin, TX : Military Millionaires, LLC, 2019.

p. ; cm.

ISBN13: 978-0-9600865-0-4

1. Veterans--United States--Finance, Personal. 2. Soldiers--United States--Finance, Personal. 3. Military pensions--United States. I. Title.

UB357.H36 2019
362.8682--dc23   2019930098

Project Coordination by Jenkins Group Inc.
www.bookpublishing.com

Cover design by Eric Tufford
Interior design by Yvonne Fetig Roehler

Printed in the United States of America
23 22 21 20 19 • 5 4 3 2 1

To the families of the
United States military.

"Thanks Mom"

CONTENTS

HOW TO USE THIS BOOK

The book you're holding in your hand, or perhaps reading on a screen, is not a treasure map. It's not a big old magic bean. But it can change your life—with your determination, perseverance, and a little discipline. But not too much determination, perseverance, and discipline. Building a healthy financial profile should not be a punishment. The long, gradual construction of a comfortable retirement should not mean a life of denial. This book's goal is not to lead you to give up everything you want and need; the goal is to help you get everything you want and need—without a lifetime of suffering to do it.

Basic Training for Personal Military Finance: Investment Strategies to Put Your Military Pay on Active Duty is built around real-life stories straight from the mouths of real-life veterans—and some service members who might still be on active duty. They tell us, in their own words, what they've learned about personal finance—both the good and the bad. They tell us about mistakes they've made so you can avoid making the same mistakes. They tell us about the good things they've done with their finances so you can do them too, if you so choose. Their stories help me, a veteran myself, bring in basic and more advanced aspects of personal finance.

You can pick and choose what you need from this book. Maybe you just want to know what to do with your enlistment or basic training money. Maybe you just want to get out of credit card debt. Maybe you're just looking for long-range retirement investment strategies. But if you're interested in any of these topics, I'll bet my honorable discharge you'll find other sections of the book helpful and interesting. I tell many stories in the book, among them my own. In these stories, you'll learn what people in situations similar to yours have done. Hopefully, understanding their successes and failures will empower you to make good choices.

Perhaps you entered the military thinking that a certain type of lifestyle and certain level of financial success were out of your reach. Not true. Reading this book can help you attain financial goals you might have thought were impossible.

My intent is to educate you, the active military service member, about the enormous advantages that can be gained from establishing a financial savings plan early in your career. I also hope to help you determine how to strike a balance between irresponsible spending and the peace of mind that a financial savings plan can offer.

As a serviceman or servicewoman in the U.S. military, you can use this book to explore your economic potential. If you want to learn how to create your own long-term financial plan while avoiding the numerous pitfalls along the way, this book is for you.

Happily, as a service member, you have the ability to accumulate a substantial amount of money for your retirement. Serving in the U.S. military starting at an early age can be the financial opportunity of a lifetime. By learning how to handle your finances at the beginning stages of your career, you can create a financially secure future in less time and with less effort than the average civilian citizen.

Imagine, in addition to serving proudly in the United States military, you also have the opportunity to position yourself to retire earlier than the average civilian. As you read, a clear picture will emerge of how making conservative monetary adjustments to your lifestyle now can substantially impact your personal finances in the future.

Applying this vital information early in your military career will allow you to stabilize your finances and promote a significant quality of life for both you and your family.

Specifically, this book will:

- Help you eliminate the mystery of the unknown in terms of your financial future
- Aid you in making informed financial decisions
- Help you overcome financial obstacles you might be facing right now
- Help you avoid financial pitfalls in the future
- Inspire you to keep moving toward your financial goals
- Assist you in exploring your potential financial prosperity
- Help you ensure a sustainable quality of life

Basic Training for Personal Military Finance is intended to be used as an educational reference. By no means does it offer specific advice on how to invest your hard-earned military pay. Rather, I hope you will use the book to educate yourself about time-proven investment tools, techniques, theories, and strategies with the goal of sharpening your understanding and strengthening your belief that you can in fact attain financial security and build wealth. My methods of teaching include definitions of financial terms, mathematical demonstrations of financial concepts, and anecdotal stories from actual members of the U.S. military.

These anecdotes are based on my observations during four years of military service in addition to stories submitted by members of the U.S. military. After my honorable discharge in 2007, I found myself thinking about the limited discussions of personal finance that occurred overseas and how more in-depth discussions could have positively influenced many young lives. I realized that most soldiers simply don't have access to the information that will allow them to make sound financial decisions. That's when I decided to write this book.

In the military, we learn our jobs during basic and advanced individual training by methods that include repetition. The information you need to achieve financial security is deliberately repeated in different ways throughout this book. My expectation is that you will become clear about the concepts and convinced of their validity as you read.

Who is this book for? It's for everyone serving in the military but especially for potential recruits or new enlistees who are interested in learning how to invest their money intelligently. *Basic Training for Personal Military Finance* covers the elementary information everyone needs to be financially literate, but an important part of the book concentrates on the many special provisions that give military personnel special financial advantages that most of the general public never hears about.

All the financial examples in the book use simple arithmetic without consideration of fluctuating markets, taxes, or other factors that could significantly reduce or increase the numerical gains in the illustrations given. All examples are exactly that: examples. They are used only to emphasize the importance of investing as early as possible. It's imperative to remember that a market's past performance does not guarantee future returns.

Basic Training for Personal Military Finance also includes the latest on new investment tools, laws, and strategies. However, that information can and does change without notice due to legislation and policy changes regarding investing, taxes, military investment options, etc.

The information presented here and elsewhere can quickly become outdated if economic shifts drive interest rates up or down or if different branches of the military change the rules and opportunities of various saving or retirement programs.

Currently, the U.S. military offers a Blended Retirement System (BRS). I highly recommend that you contact your chain of command or military finance office to learn as much as possible about this system. This book offers guidance, but check with authorities in and out of the military to make sure you have the most recent information.

Again, I do not claim any professional expertise regarding specific investments. Novice investors should seek professional financial advice to ensure they are making fully informed decisions as well as complying with current tax laws and other pertinent statutes. *Basic Training for Personal Military Finance* is just a starting point. It's designed to help you learn enough now to get started while encouraging you to continue learning.

The concepts in this book are simple: reduce debt quickly, begin saving early, increase the amounts placed in savings from time to time, invest wisely, and, most importantly, take advantage of the unique financial opportunities offered by serving in the military. When all is said and done, it's up to you to build your own financial stability and pave the way for your own comfortable retirement, and you need to start now. *Basic Training for Personal Military Finance* brings awareness of the momentous potential you have to take control of your finances, create your own investment portfolio, build wealth, and live the quality of life you deserve as a member of the U.S. military.

A final note: this book is different from the typical investing book. Some books emphasize greed along the lines of "The one with the most toys wins." That's not the approach here. We military people emphasize service and doing the right thing. We take care of others—our families, friends, community, and country. We make the world a better place. But taking care of others, and the world, starts with taking care of ourselves. If we make the right financial moves, then we won't have to depend on others to take care of us. What's more, we will be in a position to do more to take care of others.

The one who makes the world a better place is the real winner. That's you.

CHAPTER 1

THE MILITARY, MONEY, AND YOU

L et's start by meeting three pretty typical military personnel. They are very different people with different personalities. They serve in different branches of the service, are at different stages of their lives and careers, and have different outlooks on life and what they expect to get out of it. The main thing they have in common is their military service, but they're all pretty typical of the types of military people you know and have served with.

I've met a lot of these folks, learned from them, and sometimes helped them learn things too. Looking at their issues, ways of coping, at what has worked for them, at what hasn't worked, and at what they can pass along to the rest of us can make our own lives easier and better.

PRIVATE JAMES ERICKSON

Private James Erickson, United States Army, knew the first thing he wanted to do after basic training: buy a brand new car.

We met during basic and were assigned to the same initial duty station. Since Private Erickson was 18 and I had already completed a bachelor's degree in finance, he regarded me, as did many of the young guys in basic, as something of an old man. They were used to me asking them about their plans, and some of them had begun seeking my thoughts on personal finance and simple investments.

The first Saturday at our initial duty station, I was in uniform, assigned to Charge of Quarters (CQ), and posted to the front desk of our barracks. Off duty, Private Erickson stopped to talk, as he'd frequently done during basic. He and I often engaged in long, rambling discussions.

On this particular day, running into each other on our first post, I asked if he had any big plans post-basic. He sure did. He knew exactly what he was he was going to do.

"Gonna buy myself a brand new car," he boldly stated. "Why shouldn't I? I just completed basic training in the U.S. military, and I deserve a gift. I even saw a television commercial for a dealership that finances 100% for active duty service members. Better yet, I'll use my enlistment bonus and cash I saved during basic training as a down payment."

"What? Hold on a minute. Think about what you're doing," I said.

"No way. I'm going to the dealership right now."

And that's exactly what Private Erickson did.

That evening, still on CQ duty, I received a phone call.

It was Private Erickson, calling from outside our barracks. Looking out the window, I saw him waving from a brand new luxury SUV and calling me from his stylish new cell phone.

"That must have cost forty grand. How are you going to pay for it?" I asked.

"A bank gave me a loan for only $629.00 a month over the next six years. How cool is that?"

"That's ridiculous. Do you know how much that is going to end up costing you? Have you thought about how you're going to afford to keep it on the road? What about all the other costs like maintenance and insurance? How cool will you be when it's necessary to ask the bank for gas money?" I replied.

Erickson stared at me with the puzzled look of man who knew he should have some answers but didn't.

I wanted to go on. I wanted to explain that the vehicle had already depreciated in value and he now owed more than it was worth, but I held back. He'd find out the hard truth soon enough. Indeed, the look on Erickson's face told me he was already beginning to realize his purchase might not have been such a wise investment after all.

SERGEANT MAJOR DENNIS AUSTIN

The chow hall was crowded that morning at our post in Mosul, Iraq. Holding his breakfast tray in one hand, Sergeant Major Dennis Austin strolled through the crowd, looking for a place to sit. The sleeves of his uniform were covered in dust and the skin around his eyes had distinct rings where his goggles had protected them from the filthy soot in the air, but his torso was clean where his body armor had kept away the dirt and grime of the inner city of Mosul.

He pulled out the empty chair directly across from Private Erickson and me and sat down without ceremony. "Relax. As you were. Enjoy your breakfast," he instructed.

The sergeant major had joined our company on a mission the night before. We'd only been in Iraq a few weeks, and I wanted to make conversation.

"Sergeant Major Austin, this chow is pretty good," I began.

I was surprised by his response. "You know," he told us, "back stateside, it's not uncommon for a fast-food lunch to cost as much as 10 bucks. Over the past 29 years, I have contributed nearly $90,000 toward my retirement plan just from eating at the chow hall or packing my own lunch."

"That's great, Sergeant Major," I said. I was interested in finances, but we were halfway across the world. This wasn't the time and place, right?

Wrong.

The Sergeant Major leaned forward, stating, "No, you don't get it, son."

He spoke in a gruff, gravelly tone seasoned after decades as an enlistee. I stopped munching on my bacon.

He continued, "Since this is my last deployment and I'm about to retire, I'm attempting to pass on my personal finance experiences to as many of you younger recruits as I can. I'm sharing this with you not to boast about my own personal wealth. I'm telling you to make you aware of the tremendous financial advantage you have at your age. By investing your pay early and exploiting the amount of time you have on your side, your savings could grow to a much greater amount than you perhaps realize."

"Roger, Sergeant Major," I answered. I lowered my bacon and paid more respect.

"Check this out," the raspy sergeant major continued, again leaning toward us to ensure our attention. "A brand new E-1 now earns around $1,500 per month upon enlistment. After completing basic training, he or she already has $6,000 cash to salt away. Some privates are only 17 years old. Did you know that by the time that 17-year-old kid is 58, that same $6,000 could be worth over $60,000 if invested wisely? And that's without adding another penny."

"Wow, I had no idea," Private Erickson chimed in, looking bewildered. He'd already used that same money as the down payment on his brand new SUV.

The sergeant major continued, "I was the oldest of eight kids in our family. We grew up below the poverty line in rural Arkansas. My parents worked dusk 'til dawn on our small farm and took jobs when they were available in a nearby factory to feed us kids and pay the bills. Hungry and without a penny in my pocket, I proudly enlisted in the U.S. Army as an infantryman when I was 18. Next year, when I retire, I'll have nearly $400,000 in cash saved up in different investment tools, some of which are only available to those serving in the military. Those same tools are available to you."

Sitting at the table with the sergeant major, I realized I was used to talking to younger, less educated soldiers about the wisdom of saving early. Compared to them, I was seasoned, but this conversation felt like a different ball game. I was excited. I needed to know more from this man. A lot more. "How is that possible, Sergeant Major?" I asked, thinking of the many soldiers I knew who were flat broke.

"I immediately formed a savings plan after my enlistment," he replied. "My plan was simple, and I believe that's why it's been so successful. Beginning in 1976, I was able to save $200 per month. I was young, unfamiliar with even having any money. I was way too busy training as an E-2 infantryman to take the time to explore investment options, so I just placed the money in a mutual fund recommended by a captain at my unit's financial office. I have used this same mutual fund throughout my entire military career because of its conservative risk and consistent earning potential. As the years passed, I gradually increased my monthly savings. Currently, I deposit about $1,600 per month."

"It must have been hard not spending that money, Sergeant Major," Private Erickson said, no doubt thinking about the $629.00 a month he was paying for an SUV sitting back home in a friend's garage, unused. I wondered if Private Erickson might be asking himself how much money he might have had in the future if he'd invested in something other than a depreciating vehicle that he wasn't even driving.

"Yes, I made some sacrifices along the way," Sergeant Major Austin acknowledged, "but whatever it was I managed to get by without will certainly make my life more enjoyable next year when I retire. Hell, I'll only be 50 years old. Based on today's pay scale, the combat pay you guys receive during deployment, and generous reenlistment bonuses, you could achieve the same goal in considerably less time. If you two grunts have any sense, you'll take this information to heart and begin your own financial plans today."

I nodded and glanced over at my buddy, who was looking a little less puzzled and a little more remorseful.

THE PETTY OFFICERS COOPER

Mr. and Mrs. Cooper were in their mid 20s and happily married. They were both petty officers second class serving in the U.S. Navy with a combined monthly income of nearly $5,000. Because of their ability to save money by living in military housing, they rarely spent even half of their monthly paychecks. They simply directed the remaining $2,000 to $3,000 into a diversified investment portfolio that consisted primarily of the Thrift Savings Plan offered through the military. They also had a few other conservative investments including a Roth IRA, two index funds, mutual funds, and certificates of deposit. For years, they had lived a financially conservative lifestyle and focused on enjoying the simple things in life.

They both planned to achieve the rank of senior chief petty officer prior to retiring from the navy. If they succeeded, they'd have a substantial retirement plan to be proud of. They were open to considering other careers after serving in the navy, but these would be things they wanted to do, not things they had to do because they needed the money.

~

Think about these three examples. Think about the way you regard your money and your future. As these stories indicate, a stable financial status and a comfortable retirement aren't the result of doing just one thing. Financial stability and comfort are the result of doing lots of different things.

We'll visit these many things in the following pages and examine the various aspects of financial management that will help you, a member of the U.S. military, achieve financial prosperity: setting goals, making plans, budgeting, saving, spending, avoiding debt, reducing debt, basic investing, next-level investing, seeking professional advice, and building wealth.

CHAPTER 2

PERSONAL
FINANCE
IS PERSONAL

s the three anecdotes below reveal, personal finance is just that—personal.

STORY ONE

A newly married military couple found that their blended family with three kids was working well. Everybody got along, but there was one wrinkle—money. It seemed like they were earning enough, given their two salaries and assorted benefits, but they didn't seem to be managing their funds very well. It was the only area of tension between them.

STORY TWO

On the other side of the world, a 14-year-old living with his folks on a base in Germany wanted his own spending money. His parents made sure he had everything he needed and gave him a modest allowance, but he felt he needed to know more about money—and he needed more money—to do what he wanted over the next few years, including going away to college.

STORY THREE

In the American Midwest, a young guy who had been to college and gotten a decent job working in the insurance industry enlisted in the U.S. Army after the September 11, 2001, terrorist attacks. He was fit, and he loved his country. There was no reason not to sign up. From his first day in basic training and many times during his four years in the military, he was surprised at how little some of his comrades knew about money. He decided he'd try to help them understand basic money management as long as it didn't seem like he was butting into their business.

$\sim$

Personal finance is personal. That's what this book is all about. I can list financial terms and definitions and give examples of how you can earn, save, and spend wisely so that you end up with a lot bigger nest egg than you ever imagined, but none of that matters unless it aligns with your personal needs and desires, your capabilities, and your limitations. Personal finance, at least in this book, encompasses more than finances. The point is not simply to acquire more money. The point is to give you the opportunity to create a comfortable and secure life and quality lifestyle as you define it.

I'll get to facts, figures, concepts, and examples soon enough, but first I want to finish the three stories I started above. Unlike many of the other anecdotes that appear in these pages, these stories don't offer any groundbreaking lessons, but they will introduce you to the personal side of personal finance and explain why we all need to think about ourselves, our money, and each other.

STORY ONE REVISITED

Let's take a second look at the newly married couple, both on their second marriage, doing the Brady Bunch thing. The kids weren't a problem—his young son got the big sisters he'd always wanted, and her girls got the little brother they'd always wanted. The husband and wife got along well too. Their only conflict, simmering just beneath the surface—involved money. He was a spender. "Man toys," he told me. "Cars, boats, guns, basement tools, yard tools, especially if they have motors." She was a saver. She clipped coupons. She went clothes shopping a grand total of once during their first year of marriage and bought a bunch of stuff that he thought looked great on her—all for under $100.

But, gradually, their opposing viewpoints began to color their relationship. She never said anything, but he knew she thought his spending was a mistake, especially when he blew his paycheck on a new toy and she had to cover the rent and groceries and everything else from her paycheck. He started spending more impulsively and not even telling her, since he knew she'd object. In response, she began spending less, depriving herself and the rest of the family to make up for what he'd spent, but the less she saved, the more she beat herself up and worried. They never talked about it, but they each began to feel resentful. He didn't know what to do, and then one day she told him they had to talk.

"It was rough at the time, but today I'm so thankful she told me she wanted to have a serious talk about our goals as a family," he said. "I said I wanted a used Mustang some guy across town was selling. She said she wanted a nice family vacation. We made lists. I wanted stuff for myself. She wanted stuff for the family. It was like she'd hit me over the head with a baseball bat. I saw the light. I was being selfish."

His wife made another list showing him what they spent during the year. They had to buy back-to-school clothes and supplies in August. They had to save for Thanksgiving dinner in the fall, gifts at Christmas, and birthdays scattered throughout the year. In March, they'd get a little bump in income from their tax refund. In the spring, they'd figure out the summer vacation and start saving for it. There could be room for a Mustang, but it needed to be planned, just like everything else.

"Building that roadmap to success made me realize just how much my wife loved me," the husband said. "From that day on, we have been having weekly meetings, maybe just 10 or 15 minutes, going over where we are and where we want to be. My advice to you, whether you're a spender or a saver, is to get the conversation started. It's an amazing journey, traveling on the same road."

STORY TWO REVISITED

The teenager living on base in Germany with his parents had what he needed, but like many teenagers, what he thought he needed was sometimes different from what his parents thought he needed. He wanted some financial independence. At age 14, he started working in the base store, bagging groceries for cash tips. He mostly spent the cash when he got it, but gradually he began to see that if he salted some money away, he could afford bigger and better things.

His dad was sent to another base in Texas when the boy was 16. In Texas, the boy looked for work off the base. He got a job in construction and began making a little more than minimum wage. Every two weeks, when that paycheck came in, he felt rich. He learned a lot about civil engineering and about how contract jobs work. He decided he wanted to go to college and study engineering, but his folks could only afford to send him to the local community college. His parents agreed to work with him and see what they could do to get him to a four-year college. They helped him plan a budget and figure out how to save some of his construction earnings. They helped him plot out the cost of four years of college. They helped him apply for scholarships and loans—good loans, not the kind that rip off college students—and look for colleges with engineering programs that were also a good value. His parents also found they could tap military programs providing financial aid to sons and daughters.

When I first encountered this kid, he wasn't a kid any more. "I'm 18," he told me. "I'm on my way to a four-year university to study engineering in the fall. I look back at my friends, and most of them are going to community college. That's what I would be doing if my parents hadn't helped me chart this path. I'm not going to let them down."

STORY THREE REVISITED

Who's that third individual? The guy who enlisted in the U.S. Army as an infantryman after graduating from college with a degree in finance?

That's me, the author of this book. In addition to all the stories I gathered from veterans and active military personnel for *Basic Training for Personal Military Finance*, I decided to share my own personal story.

After high school, I earned a bachelor's degree in finance. Upon graduation, I accepted a position with a Fortune 500 insurance company. It was a good job, but when 9/11 occurred, I felt compelled to serve in the military like my dad and grandfathers. I served four years, including 16 months as an infantry team leader in Iraq.

I was a full decade older than most of the guys I served with. Perhaps that was why I was concerned about how little thought or planning—either short range or long term—went into their financial decisions. I'd been no different at their age, and I could relate to their impulsive spending habits. As far back as basic training, I realized that their lack of enthusiasm for saving and investing their pay was more an outgrowth of their lack of knowledge than a lack of interest. The new recruits simply didn't know how advantageous it would be to start saving and investing at a young age.

Meanwhile, during our combat tour in Iraq, these young enlistees began to see their bank accounts accumulate cash they'd never had before. They loved talking about how they were going to spend it. Some were already spending it. One purchased a brand new car online to be picked up upon returning to U.S. Another did the same with a new motorcycle. Since I was "the old man" with a bachelor's degree in finance, a few asked my advice on how to invest their pay. This question seemed way too complex at the time, so I replied, "Just save it for now, and we'll talk about it when we get home." After all, we had a job to focus on. I wanted to educate the soldiers about personal finance, but my priority was our mission in Iraq.

When we returned from deployment, I realized my mistake. My plan to provide financial education upon our return wasn't going to work. I hadn't realized that the majority of those I'd worked with for the past 16 months would re-deploy to other units and I would quickly lose track of them. I had envisioned getting groups of soldiers together, maybe in a classroom setting, all of them interested in learning how to wisely invest their money, but that didn't happen. Meanwhile, the privates' enthusiasm to invest was short lived, and they spent their saved money just like everybody else. Sadly, those who had once been interested in learning about investing succumbed to the enticement of modern-day luxuries. Soon, their cash was gone.

I realized I had to do something. Most of the soldiers were very young, just kids, really. They weren't trying to waste money or scuttle their financial futures or ruin their chances of ever having a comfortable retirement. They weren't trying to be poor or stay poor all their lives. In most cases, they simply didn't know any better. Many people who are drawn to military service haven't had the advantage of a college education or an upbringing among people who are sophisticated about saving and investing.

I was fortunate to have parents, aunts and uncles, grandparents, bosses, teachers, and professors pass on their understanding and appreciation of finances to me, but many serving in the military never receive that kind of money-friendly upbringing and aren't prepared to fend for themselves. They need guidance to learn how to handle their money and to plan for a comfortable retirement in a fast-changing world. They simply haven't been shown, either in school or anywhere else, what's involved in making basic sound financial decisions. They simply don't know what's possible.

Thanks to many casual, friendly conversations, I realized what a service it would be to pass along some of the basics I had been taught about saving, spending, investing, and being a good financial citizen to all of those serving in the U.S. armed forces. That's why I decided to write *Basic Training for Personal Military Finance.*

Personal finance is personal, and every U.S. service member deserves a chance to learn how to put their money to work and create their own financially secure future.

CHAPTER 3

DOLLARS AND SENSE: SOME MONEY BASICS

*M*arine Corps Regiment Commander Colonel David Walsh didn't have a million dollars in the bank when he retired, but he sure felt like a millionaire. He explained that his savings consisted of nearly $300,000. From a portion of that, he would earn approximately 2.25% annual interest in low-risk money-market funds and approximately 1.75% in CDs that were insured by the Federal Deposit Insurance Corporation (FDIC). In addition, after retirement, he would begin to receive his annual pension, nearly $40,000.

Colonel Walsh realized that the interest from his low-risk investments, when added to his annual pension, equaled the amount of interest he would have earned if he'd had a million dollars cash in the bank. The icing on the cake was that he'd saved an additional $200,000 *over his 30-year military career so that he could pay cash for the construction of a new home upon his retirement.*

~

As individuals, we all envision our retirements differently. The vision of Colonel Walsh is particularly interesting. With a long-term outlook, his philosophy was that just a fraction of a service member's paycheck could snowball into a substantial amount—if it was handled properly.

Colonel Walsh didn't claim to be a financial expert, but now that he's settled into his new home on his horse farm in Kentucky, he's no doubt pleased with the foresight he used to accomplish his goals.

"Foresight" is defined as perceiving the significance and nature of events before they've occurred; care in providing for the future; and the act of looking forward.

Military personnel like Colonel Walsh who have the ability to envision their livelihoods in the future are likely to achieve financial success. Foresight can assist investors in achieving both short- and long-term goals and motivate them while they do so.

In other words, individuals who have the ability to envision where they will be in five, 10, 30, or even 50 years find it much easier to adjust their current lifestyles and reach their goals. Nobody can actually see the future, of course, but we can all try, and that often helps make it come true.

Designing a lifelong structured investment plan can seem pretty overwhelming. For many, the most daunting phase is getting started. But once you've mastered the basics, you will discover that an effective investment portfolio isn't so challenging after all. It's merely a matter of simple arithmetic.

Some of these early explanations might seem basic, but readers who are new to these concepts shouldn't be left behind.

PRINCIPAL

The principal is the original amount of money you deposit into an interest-earning savings account.

INTEREST

Interest is a fee paid to a depositor by a lending institution such as a bank or credit union on borrowed capital. The concept is that the financial institution is "borrowing" money from you. The interest can be thought of as "rent" on the money you deposit in a bank or credit union. The amount of interest applied to the principal is referred to as the interest rate.

In other words, interest is money one person or institution pays to borrow money from another. It's usually expressed in annual percentage terms. If you borrow $100 from me at 5% annual interest for a year, at the end of the year, you are obligated to pay me back the $100 plus the 5% annual interest—$5—so you hand me $105.

In effect, you rent my $100 for a year to use for whatever you want, maybe to buy seeds for a crop, an engagement ring, a musical instrument, or whatever. Paying the $5 in interest allows you to make your purchase or investment right away instead of waiting until you have saved up the $100. These interest-paying, interest-charging agreements are legal contracts signed by both the lender and the borrower. The lender earns passive income for loaning out the money. In this instance, the lender makes $5 without lifting a finger.

Banks are in the business of both paying and charging interest. If you deposit money in a savings account, the bank typically pays interest on it. Historically, bank interest rates fluctuate dramatically but pay as high as 3% to 6% a year, though sometimes more in inflationary periods. (Inflation is when the cost of things goes up, often for complicated economic reasons. Obviously, things cost more today than when you were a kid. There can be many reasons why something costs more, but it's often attributed to inflation.)

Instead of the typical 3% to 6% annual interest on savings accounts banks have historically paid, interest rates have been much lower in the twenty-first century. Many banks today pay as little as one-tenth of 1% a year in interest on their savings accounts. A savings account—or any other type of account—that pays 2% a year could be very attractive to savers in 2019.

Banks also charge interest when they lend money, often for car loans, business loans, home improvement loans, or mortgages. In effect, local banks pay you a little interest on the money you deposit and then loan that money to others at a higher interest rate.

If you buy a house for $100,000 with a 30-year mortgage at 4%, your monthly payments (360 payments over 360 months) are going to add up to about $172,000 by the end of the 30 years. Is it worth it to pay an additional $72,000 over the sale price? Yeah, probably. You get to live in the house for 30 years. You're not paying rent all those years. And at the end of 30 years, you own the house, which by now might well be worth a lot more than $172,000. Indeed, historically, home ownership has been the cornerstone of financial stability for many American families.

Half a century ago, when banking was much simpler, a joke was told about 3-6-3 bankers: they pay 3% on deposits, collect 6% on loans, and are on the golf course by 3:00 o'clock.

Lending institutions offer two different types of interest: simple interest and compound interest.

Simple Interest

With simple interest, the amount of the deposit doesn't change. The interest earned is paid directly to the depositor at the end of each determined interval of time. This interest is not added to the principal (the initial deposit). It is given to the depositor rather than placed in the account. If the owner of the savings account never adds or withdraws funds after making the initial deposit, he or she will be paid the same amount of interest each interval.

The following table shows how simple interest accumulates over 10 years. Let's say you deposit $1,000 in a savings account at a local credit union. The account earns 3% interest annually.

Years Passed	Account Balance	Percent Interest	Interest Earned
1	$1,000.00	3%	$30.00
2	$1,000.00	3%	$30.00
3	$1,000.00	3%	$30.00
4	$1,000.00	3%	$30.00
5	$1,000.00	3%	$30.00
6	$1,000.00	3%	$30.00
7	$1,000.00	3%	$30.00
8	$1,000.00	3%	$30.00
9	$1,000.00	3%	$30.00
10	$1,000.00	3%	$30.00
Total	$1,000.00		$300.00

At the end of each year, the $30 is paid to you, and you may reinvest it or choose not to. You can withdraw your money, or part of it, and do something else with it if you like.

Compound Interest

With compound interest, the interest that is earned over a set period of time such as a quarter of a year is left in the account. This additional money is included in future compounding along with the initial deposit. With compound interest, future interest is earned on the original principal *plus* the interest from the previous quarter.

In other words, compounding occurs when accumulated interest is declared to be part of the principal. In this way, the interest earned each quarter is figured on a larger amount of money than the quarter before. If you recall, earnings in a simple interest account are paid directly to the owner of the account and aren't included in future compounding.

Certain factors affect the amount of money earned. First of all, the amount earned depends on the frequency with which interest is compounded. It might be compounded annually, quarterly, monthly, or daily. In order to accurately define the amount to be paid under a legal contract, your financial institution will clearly specify the interest rate and the frequency with which it is compounded when you open an account.

The table on the next page offers an example of compound interest over 10 years. Again, let's say you have deposited $1,000 in a local credit union at 3% interest.

Years Passed	Account Balance	Percent Interest	Interest Earned
1	$1,000.00	3%	$30.00
2	$1,030.00	3%	$30.09
3	$1,060.09	3%	$32.64
4	$1,092.73	3%	$32.79
5	$1,125.52	3%	$33.77
6	$1,159.29	3%	$34.78
7	$1,194.07	3%	$35.82
8	$1,229.89	3%	$36.90
9	$1,266.79	3%	$38.01
10	$1,304.80	3%	$39.15
Total	$1,343.95		$343.95

In this example, $343.95 is earned due to the power of compound interest.

Simple versus Compound Interest

Let's take one last look at simple and compound interest. The following tables (continued on the next page) show these examples side by side.

SIMPLE INTEREST

Years Passed	Account Balance	Interest Earned
1	$1,000.00	$30.00
2	$1,000.00	$30.00
3	$1,000.00	$30.00

4	$1,000.00	$30.00
5	$1,000.00	$30.00
6	$1,000.00	$30.00
7	$1,000.00	$30.00
8	$1,000.00	$30.00
9	$1,000.00	$30.00
10	$1,000.00	$30.00
Total	**$1,000.00**	**$300.00**

COMPOUND INTEREST

Years Passed	Account Balance	Interest Earned
1	$1,000.00	$30.00
2	$1,030.00	$30.09
3	$1,060.09	$32.64
4	$1,092.73	$32.79
5	$1,125.52	$33.77
6	$1,159.29	$34.78
7	$1,194.07	$35.82
8	$1,229.89	$36.90
9	$1,266.79	$38.01
10	$1,304.80	$39.15
Total	**$1,343.95**	**$343.95**

When you compare the $300.00 earned with the simple interest account to the $343.95 earned with the compound interest account over the same 10-year period, you see the additional $43.95 earned and gain a visual perspective of the mathematics involved.

The Rule of 72

The "Rule of 72" is a method for determining how fast money grows when earning a given interest rate. To use it, you simply divide 72 by your interest rate to find out how many years it will take your money to double.

Let's use an 8% interest rate as an example: 72 ÷ 8 = 9 years. So, it will take nine years for your investment to double. This is merely an approximation, and it starts to break down at rates above 10%, but this gives you a general idea of how the rule of 72 works.

THE TIME VALUE OF MONEY AND THE POWER OF COMPOUNDING

Albert Einstein said that compound interest is one of the greatest mathematical concepts of our time. Compounding has also been called the eighth wonder of the world. Why? The power of compound interest can turn even a modest amount of money into a staggering sum that most people find unbelievable.

Remember that $100 I lent you at 5% annual interest at the beginning of this chapter? Let's say you keep that money for two years. When you repay me after two years, you don't repay me an additional $10, or $5 for each year. No, you pay the first 5%, or $5, and then also 5% of $100 plus $5, which is $5.25. Therefore, the total interest you pay is $10.25. That makes the total you pay—the interest plus the principal (the original amount)—$110.25.

The time value of money is defined as the value of money, figuring in a given amount of interest, earned over a given amount of time. The time value of money is the central concept in finance theory. Lucky you—by beginning your financial plan today, time is on your side!

PUT YOUR MONEY TO WORK FOR YOU

As the saying goes, smart people put their money to work for them. How do they do it? It can be as simple as storing money in a savings account. Deposits in a savings account earn interest. The more you save and the longer you save, the harder your money works for you by earning interest.

For example, if you place a $1 bill in a box every day for 40 years, at the end of that period, you will have accumulated $14,600.00 (1×365×40=$14,600).

But what would happen if you deposited that same single $1 bill in a savings account that earned 2% interest? Through the power of compounding, that same amount would earn an additional $7,765.23 for a grand total of $22,365.23. This example reveals how the expression "putting your money to work for you" came about. The power of compounding creates what is known as passive income.

A CLOSER LOOK AT THE TIME VALUE OF MONEY

When it comes to investing, time might very well be the most valuable element of your investment plan. By extension, the mismanagement of time can have a devastating effect on your money.

The time value of money is based on the premise that an investor will likely prefer to receive a fixed amount of money today rather than the same amount at some point in the future. The philosophy is that a dollar today is worth more than a dollar tomorrow; a dollar today can earn interest until the time you would have received the money in the future, which equals a larger sum. Therefore, common sense tells us that it's better to receive money sooner and invest it in order to take advantage of the accumulating interest.

For example, assuming a 3% interest rate, $100 that you invest today will be worth $103 in one year. But $100 that you receive today may be the equivalent of only $97 a year ago due to the interest opportunity you lost along with inflation.

THE MILITARY ADVANTAGE

To see the tremendous impact of starting to save early, let's look at the value of time from another perspective.

Consider a college graduate who, after paying off all outstanding student loans by age 29, manages to faithfully save $4,200.00 a year. If the college grad is fortunate enough to earn a 5.7% annual percentage rate (APR) until he or she chooses to retire at the age of 65, it might be possible to accumulate $468,409.01.

On the other hand, with the ability to annually invest the same amount of $4,200.00 at the age of 18, an E1 private would amass $923,783.48 by age 65. This is the dramatic effect of just a few extra years of compound interest.

This example is based on a 5.7% annual percentage rate of return, which is pretty close to an average return for the last 100 years for the typical investor. While such a consistent return is by no means guaranteed, this example clarifies how saving as much as you can as early as you can tremendously impacts your ultimate goal.

By now, I hope that the noticeable advantage military recruits have to save during these early years is apparent. These are the same years that often unexpectedly slip past the average civilian. By creating a savings plan today and taking advantage of investing early, service members have additional time for interest to compound and thus a distinct advantage.

THE BOTTOM LINE WITH COMPOUND INTEREST

The younger the investor, the more distant retirement age is. The more distant retirement age is, the more advantageous compound interest is. That's it. That's the bottom line. Now when you hear your fellow service members say, "Oh, I'm young, I have plenty of time to worry about retirement," you can jump in and educate them on their most valuable asset—time.

In case you're still not convinced, let's look at one final example. To accrue $1,000,000 by age 65, a 45-year-old chief executive officer of a Fortune 500 company who has not yet begun to save would have to set aside $2,164.31 every single month, assuming a 6% APR.

How much would an 18-year-old private serving in the U.S. military need to save to have roughly the same amount by age 65? Only $319.30 a month, assuming a 6% APR!

Now it's clear why saving and investing your hard-earned military pay as early as possible is such an advantage.

SAVINGS AND CHECKING ACCOUNTS

The two types of bank accounts are savings and checking.

Savings Accounts

Savings accounts are accounts maintained by retail financial institutions (banks or credit unions) that return a specified interest rate on your deposited funds. A savings account can provide the essential framework for your investment plans while earning interest, and it insures your deposits up to $250,000.

A savings account is the easiest and safest way to begin earning interest on your hard-earned military pay. It's a simple tool that offers a solid foundation for your long-term financial plan. Once placed in a savings account, your money immediately goes to work for you.

Checking Accounts

A checking account is a deposit account at a financial institution into which you deposit funds for the purpose of security. In addition, you can write checks, withdraw money from an ATM, and make purchases with debit cards.

When opening a checking account, make sure that:

- The account is FDIC insured
- You have unlimited withdrawals
- There are no fees on withdrawals
- You have ATM access to the checking account
- The account offers a competitive interest rate
- There are no minimum balance requirements
- There are no fees for falling below a minimum balance

A minimum balance requirement refers to the fact that some banks charge a fee if your balance falls below their selected minimum balance. Instead of using this bank, search for one that has no minimum balance requirement unless it pays a higher interest rate and you're sure your account won't fall below the minimum.

It can be frustrating to withdraw money because you're facing a financial emergency and then find yourself penalized for using your own money. As always, shop around, especially for your bank.

CHAPTER 4

THE BIG PICTURE: SETTING YOUR GOALS

*I*t was a sunny afternoon, and the two young sailors were on shore leave. They were livin' large in their dress whites, fresh off the ship. They plopped down on stools in the first bar they came to, savoring their beers and talking about a future that seemed so bright, they should have been wearin' shades.

They decided to have one more beer and then head to another bar where they'd heard young ladies from nearby office buildings liked to congregate when the working day was done.

Pretty soon the two guys were talking about their futures further out—how long they wanted to serve in the U.S. Navy and what they wanted to do afterward, when their working days were done.

"I want to have a lot of money when I retire," the first sailor declared. *He sounded determined and confident he was going to be rich.*

The second sailor stated, "I want to put in my 20 years, and by the time I come out, I want to have $500,000 in assets, including an annuity and some other long-range investments, some real property, and at least $100,000 in ready cash. I want to be in a position to make a down payment on a house in a good neighborhood in my hometown, an old house that has good bones that needs some work, a fixer-upper that's a good investment. A place that might make a good family home for a long time."

~

For the first sailor, being rich is an excellent idea, but that's all it is: an idea. As a goal, it's completely ineffective because it isn't specific.

The other sailor, by contrast, has clearly stated goals with specific financial landmarks.

If you had to pick, which sailor do you think has a better chance of making his dreams come true? Which sailor has a better goal? Which sailor would you rather be?

Goals are good. Goals are necessary. Goals are the stepping stones to success for most of us. If your plan is simply to be lucky—to hope it all works out somehow—well, good luck with that.

Plans are good. We all know it, even if we aren't always good about making plans. If you have a plan, you're much more likely be successful. This is true for pretty much anything. If you have a plan for a hike in the woods, you're probably going to have the clothes and footwear you need. You're probably going to have water and snacks and you're going to know your route. You're not going to be too hot or too cold and your feet aren't going to hurt. You're not going to be thirsty or hungry. You're not going to get lost. You're going to finish in time to keep other plans you have.

We make plans for how to play games or run races or lift weights. We make plans for how to get through school and earn the degree or certification we want. We make plans for how to pass individual courses. We make plans for when to study so we can ace an exam. We need to make financial plans too, in the short term, long term, and medium term. But to make those plans, we need goals. Like the sailor who has specific goals, we need to be able to see ourselves in a future time and place, to actually envision our future selves.

Maybe you're familiar with the old trick taught by sports psychologists and life coaches to visualize yourself in your mind's eye, over and over, finishing the 10K or walking across the stage to get your diploma. As you repeat the exercise, you add details and see your vision more clearly. You're wearing your favorite running shorts and a comfortable T-shirt with your race number pinned to the front. You're wearing a gray robe and one of those mortarboard caps with a tassel hanging down. You raise your arms as you cross the finish line. You shake hands with the teacher handing out the diplomas. You wave to your friends on the sidelines, cheering you on. You wave to your family in the audience as you walk offstage with your diploma.

Envisioning the future, the more specifically the better, makes it more real to us, more possible mentally, psychologically, emotionally, and, in some cases, even more attainable physically. Your goals will sometimes change, of course, depending on the resources available to you at various times during your life. You'll need to calculate—and periodically re-calculate—your current and projected income to determine what's realistic and how you can achieve as many goals as possible.

It is much easier to devise a plan using your current and projected income if you state specific, clear goals. If you establish your goals firmly before you create a specific plan for achieving them, you might find out early on that certain goals aren't feasible—or you might discover that you can set even higher goals than you anticipated.

Start envisioning your long-term financial stability. Start way in the future with your goals for retirement. Get out a pen and paper, maybe a new little notebook that will be dedicated to your financial goals over the years, and start making a list. Or open a computer file. It's good to have your goals—flexible and changing over time—in one place for easy reference over the years.

Start by listing what you want in the future—next month, next year, in 10 years, in 20 years. Look at the big picture. What are your goals? Four and out? A second career? Twenty years in with retirement benefits? Be realistic, or at least more realistic than the sailor whose only plan was to be a millionaire someday.

When you set an ideal retirement age, there is no right or wrong answer, but avoid being unrealistic by setting a retirement age and lifestyle you know will be out of reach. Envision a lifestyle you can actually see for yourself, one that would suit you. Running a small bed and breakfast near a national park might seem very realistic if you can actually see yourself doing that. Sailing your 200-foot yacht in the Mediterranean with a year-round captain and crew might seem like a pleasant dream, but it might not be how you really see yourself in the future.

Of course, nobody can predict decades into the future, but we can set the goal line, even if it changes numerous times. Your lists can monitor and measure your progress, maybe in monthly or quarterly or annual check-ins. Your ever-evolving plan is all about keeping track, being flexible, and adjusting the plan to get to where you want to be. The point is to get the most out of what is available to you, both now, in the military, and later, once you're a civilian again.

HOW DO YOU ENVISION YOUR LIFESTYLE DURING RETIREMENT?

The first step to figuring out how much money you will need during retirement is to think about what you will be doing at that time of your life. For some people, retirement is a time to do all the things they were unable to do while working. For others, it's a time for leisure and rest. For most, it's somewhere in between.

To begin, ask yourself this simple question: "What type of lifestyle do I want to have when I stop working?" Every answer will be different. Your unique answer will determine the amount of money you will need. Maybe you have a list of things you've always wanted to do such as traveling or pursuing hobbies but you've been too busy working.

Will your retirement lifestyle increase the amount you spend? To support these costs, will you need an income greater than your monthly paycheck? Perhaps you picture yourself enjoying your free time leisurely reading books, going to the movies, and engaging in less extravagant recreational activities near home. By doing so, you might actually spend less money than you do now.

The key is to prepare a financial plan today that will support the lifestyle you anticipate in the future. If your savings plan today won't support your retirement, you might need to significantly alter your current lifestyle. If your current plan supports your future endeavors, saving money for retirement should be relatively easy for you.

HOW DO YOU MAKE SURE YOU CAN AFFORD THE LIFESTYLE YOU WANT?

That's a good question. Fortunately, the answer is simple. Your current financial plan should balance your income and your lifestyle. That's it.

For example, early in your working career, if you choose to use a large portion of your monthly income to mortgage a luxury car, far less of your money will be available for savings. The result could be a longer working career than you'd like, less money when you retire, or both. Defining and maintaining your balance is the key to reaching the goals you envision.

Determining a financial plan that works best for you is based upon knowing where your future is headed. Whether retirement is 40 years or 40 weeks away, start by mapping out some of your broader goals. As you do so, consider the following questions:

- At what age do you plan to retire?
- How much time do you have until you reach that age?
- Are you planning to retire completely or to continue working part time?
- Will your projected savings meet your needs?

After you have determined the answers to these questions, you can begin to fine-tune your plan for attaining them.

A MILLION DOLLARS SHOULD BE ENOUGH...RIGHT?

Professional advisors estimate that the average retired person requires 60% to 80% of his or her last year's working income to maintain an equivalent lifestyle after retirement. Calculating the amount of income you believe will be necessary to support your retirement lifestyle allows you to structure your current savings plan to best accomplish your goal. Figuring this out today will give you a rough estimate of how much money you really need for tomorrow.

The fact is, if you've saved a million dollars and are fortunate enough to earn between 2% and 4% interest from this sum of money, you can anticipate an income between $20,000 and $40,000 annually. Although this is a respectable amount, it only goes as far as inflation, your lifestyle, and your health will allow. Without any debt, this conservative amount might or might not provide a comfortable lifestyle. For those who envision a life of luxury, this amount will likely not be enough.

Take a look at your current expenses. If you think these will be the same once you retire, it's easy to figure out what income you will need to have later. And if you suspect you will be spending more, or less, after retirement, you can plan accordingly.

DEVELOP FORESIGHT

Take a moment to think of the purchases you have made over the past few years, both large and small. Then consider whether they were worth the money you spent on them. Be honest with yourself when asking the following questions:

- Could I have gotten by just as well purchasing a used version or perhaps a less luxurious one?
- Could I have bought a smaller amount of something rather than the supersized amount?
- Could I have avoided the more expensive name brand and purchased the generic version?

Taking the time to reflect on how you could have handled your money differently is healthy. Learning from past experiences can certainly benefit your future. Imagine if the cash from excessive spending in the past were in your bank account today, accumulating interest—what a feeling that would be!

Now, imagine yourself five years in the future. Where do you see yourself living? What kind of home or apartment do you see yourself in? How do you spend your leisure time? What do you own? Or, conversely, are you struggling in debt?

Picturing your financial situation down the road is a simple but effective approach to predicting where you will be after you make future purchases.

To develop foresight, learn from your past but don't dwell on it. Evaluate your past spending habits and recognize what you could have done differently. Then keep moving forward. That's what having superior foresight is all about.

DETERMINE YOUR GOALS

To determine your goals, you need to distinguish the things you need in life from the things you want. Once this is clear, you can define your goals. Establishing goals and preparing a plan to meet them in the short term, the medium term, and the long term will ensure that you can build a financially sound future.

Short-term goals attainable within one year might include:

- Creating a $1,000 emergency fund
- Paying off, or beginning to pay off, all credit card debt
- Reducing spending by $150 a month

Medium-term goals attainable within five years might include:

- Funding a six-month emergency savings account
- Making a down payment on a home
- Paying cash for a quality pre-owned vehicle

Long-term goals that get you where you want to be in retirement might include:

- Owning your home debt free
- Building a retirement account large enough for the interest to support you
- Having cash to pay for your children's education

These are all examples of attainable financial goals, but they won't happen on their own. Each goal requires extensive planning, conservative living, and follow-through. The good news is that with a sound strategy and the discipline to avoid costly temptations, you can attain your goals easily and with little stress.

Now that you've defined your goals, it's time to map out the route that will allow you to achieve them.

CHAPTER 5

YOUR GAME PLAN
FOR REACHING
YOUR GOALS

*H*e introduced himself as Captain Jerome Grant.

"I've served in the U.S. Coast Guard for 13 years," he told me. "Prior to my enlistment, I graduated with a bachelor's degree in mechanical engineering. Currently, I perform a relatively high-tech job as a captain piloting an HH-60J Jayhawk."

Captain Grant had a confession for me, and he admitted it was a little embarrassing: "Can you imagine performing this complex job but somehow not having the ability to balance a checkbook? Well, it's true."

He had taken an accounting course for his engineering degree, he told me, but it hadn't covered the basics of personal finance, things like establishing a budget. Eventually, Captain Grant and his wife had met with the branch manager of their bank and asked for a lesson on how to read their monthly bank statement.

It was pretty remarkable to me that the Grants would admit to their banker that they didn't know how to balance their checkbook and then be brave enough to ask for coaching.

"Soon, we realized that one of our biggest obstacles to financial security was that we didn't understand the basic concepts of investing money and the tools used to do it," Captain Grant continued. "So we decided to do something about it."

He explained, "We made an appointment with a reputable professional financial advisor who answered our questions and explained that the majority of his clients were novices just like my wife and me. He described how many of his clients had avoided investing altogether because they didn't understand how it worked."

The financial advisor gave the Grants some basic advice. "To continuously make money," he explained, "you must be financially literate."

Captain Grant and his wife started checking out personal finance books at the library. With the help of books and trusted professional advice, they began applying their new-found financial knowledge to their lifestyle. Their first step was to document their financial profile. This basically meant accounting for what they earned, what they spent, and how they spent it.

Simply knowing the resources they had available to them helped the Grants make a plan—also called a budget—and stick to it.

"We are now living well below our combined income," Captain Grant said. "We save a great deal of money with our frugal lifestyle, and we place 20% of our annual salaries into our diversified investments.

With a little luck, we plan to retire in our mid 50s, at which time we'll have accumulated more money than we ever thought possible."

⁓

Just as we need basic training for the military, we should assign ourselves basic training for our finances. We need to understand how it all works. After we set goals, we need to make a plan for getting there. This requires calculating what resources we will have now and in the future. To know what we will be able to afford, we also need to know what we spend. More specifically, we need to know when, where, why, and how we spend our money and whether we spend wisely and in line with our goals. In other words, we each need a budget, but before we can create one, we need to get organized.

What will organizing your personal finances do for you? It will:

- Ensure that your bills are paid on time
- Help you avoid late fees
- Help you avoid debt
- Instill confidence because you know you're in control
- Equip you to prepare your own tax statements
- Help you attain financial goals
- Promote confidence

On the other hand, handling your finances haphazardly can lead to:

- Loss of receipts
- Late bill payment or failure to pay bills at all
- Loss of assets, including cash
- Borrowing funds to meet obligations
- Endless searches for lost tax documentation

- Damaged credit rating
- Unnecessary frustration

If you're going to maintain financial records, including a budget, you need to be organized. It's one thing to throw all your financial information in a drawer or stack papers on a desk, but what good is that if you don't have totals? Keeping receipts from service stations won't tell you how much you've spent on gas unless you add up the bills. You've got to maintain records and keep files, especially if the Internal Revenue Service (IRS) decides to audit you.

Creating a filing system that works for you will prevent you from wasting valuable time and money. Begin by identifying any problems you recognize in your current system, if you have one. Then implement strategies to help you overcome these concerns. Add new techniques that can further streamline your record-keeping system.

The system you use will likely evolve over time, but structuring your personal finances will allow you to track your spending, organize your tax return information, and effectively store documentation. It will also allow you to create that all-important budget. If you don't have a system that works for you, or if the one you use is ineffective, read on.

THE PERSONAL BUDGET

To become financially successful, you must develop a personal budget, which is an estimation of your income and expenses over a specified period of time. Your budget can also be viewed as an individual financial plan that distributes future income toward expenses, debt, savings, and investments.

The information you need to create a budget includes past spending in addition to known future income and expense obligations. A well-planned budget will provide the framework for living within your means and will also tell you how much you can designate for savings each month. Your financial success will greatly increase after establishing a budget.

Plan on establishing your budget based upon your pay periods. Typically, service members are paid bimonthly, and bills are usually due at different times of the month. To eliminate surprises, begin by writing down each of your monthly bills.

As time goes by, you can fine tune your budget. For example, your utility bills might increase when you purchase a home. If so, you can simply increase the amount budgeted for this monthly expense.

On the other hand, your income will fluctuate when you are promoted to a higher rank, receive a re-enlistment bonus, or eliminate the debt that has been dragging you down. These surplus funds can then be added to your emergency fund or perhaps to your long-term investment portfolio.

When starting out, remember that handling your finances appropriately is part of a long-term lifestyle you want to live. In other words, your initial attempt to budget your money does not have to be perfect. Your goal should be to establish a simple budget to assure yourself that you are living within your means and not acquiring additional debt.

KEEP IT SIMPLE

When first designing your budget, use as few budget categories as possible. Some folks recommend complicated systems with lots of different categories, but when you are just beginning to get organized, I suggest keeping your method as simple as possible. With time, you'll discover that a simple budget requiring 15 to 20 minute per week can reduce stress and eliminate the need for complicated tracking schemes.

A software program can be a good way to get organized, but specialty budget software can be extremely detailed and tedious because of the extensive categorization it provides. If this occurs, users can get discouraged and give up entirely, or, even worse, fall further into debt.

CONSIDER USING A
BASIC ELECTRONIC SPREADSHEET

For many, the easiest way to establish a budget is through the use of an electronic worksheet. My basic electronic spreadsheet contains columns for income and expenses, and I've created a simple formula that adds up the totals of each column of numbers.

I start by listing my income and my monthly expenses. After considering my larger monthly expenses, I try to include just the basics such as food, gas, and general entertainment. This technique keeps me organized and takes no time at all to adjust if my income changes or new expenses occur. If a new category emerges, whether in income or expenses, I can either make it a sub-category of an existing category or create a new category.

ESTABLISH YOUR BUDGET STEP BY STEP

Follow the four steps below to establish a budget.

1. Determine your income. First, you need to confirm exactly how much income you receive each month. This includes your monthly salary as well as any additional supplemental income you receive from a second job, investments, combat pay, a housing allowance, enlistment bonuses, etc.

2. Determine your expenses. This task might prove to be more difficult since it's necessary to determine exactly how much you spend each month. Larger fixed expenses such as mortgages, vehicle payments, insurance, and utilities are simple to track. Smaller non-fixed expenses such as gas, eating in restaurants, and entertainment are more challenging. Track them for a few months and use the average to determine your expenses.

3. Calculate your surplus cash. This step determines how much you can earmark for savings each month. Simply subtract your monthly expenses, determined in step two, from your monthly income, determined in step one. The remaining amount is the amount you can save. An ideal target for savings would be 40% of your overall income. Remember, saving money is not an exact science, and you can increase or decrease the amount you save as your life circumstances change. The most important part is to begin

saving now, no matter how much or how little you can afford.

4. Establish an emergency fund. An emergency fund is intended to absorb large unanticipated expenses that come up from time to time. Examples could include:

   - An automobile collision
   - A home fire
   - An accident
   - A flood
   - Unforeseen medical expenses
   - A death in the family

   Having such a fund will prevent you from going into debt should something of this nature occur. Later in the book, I'll discuss in greater detail how to establish your emergency fund.

USE A TABLE TO OUTLINE YOUR GOALS

Using a table such as the sample table below makes it easier to set and attain goals. Once you see your goals all together on paper, it quickly becomes apparent what's feasible and what won't work within the constraints of your monthly budget. A table allows you to easily adjust the numbers to reflect your current situation, particularly if you create it in a spreadsheet.

By routinely monitoring your progress, you might find that your long-term goals are negatively affecting your ability to attain your short-term goals or vice versa. On the other hand, you might find that you're living well within your means and can set even loftier short- or long-term goals. With this information, you can readjust your funds to work to your advantage.

Financial Goal	Time Required to Reach Goal	Goal Amount	Interest Paid or Earned	Necessary Monthly Budgeted Amount
Pay off credit card balance	12 months	$2,600.00	-13%	$233.00
Pay off vehicle loan	36 months	$8,000.00	-8%	$251.00
Down payment for first home	5 years	$20,000.00	+2%	$320.00
Children's college fund	18 years	$50,000.00	+3%	$180.00
Retirement savings	30 years	$500,000.00	+4.6%	$650.00
Total Monthly Savings				$1,524.00

RUN YOUR OWN NUMBERS

To learn more about compound interest and projections based upon your savings plan, simply search "financial calculator" on the internet. Numerous sites are available that allow you to run your own numbers. Doing so will help you determine how much you need to set aside each month to reach your goals.

At the same time, running your own numbers will let you see what's truly attainable and help you become excited about your financial future. Realizing your income's potential is an excellent motivator, which makes the ability to project your income's growth potential a critical part of staying on track.

DON'T GET DISCOURAGED

As you run the numbers for a specific goal, it might become apparent that your vision of the future has a distinct possibility of becoming reality.

On the other hand, you might realize that you need to reconsider expectations that are too lofty and set your sights on more realistic objectives. If this is the case, don't get discouraged. You are very fortunate to have found out early in life that you can make adjustments and find a way to accomplish your ambitions.

Either way, you will soon discover that if you save as much as possible, as early as possible, you will be off to an excellent start.

KEEP RECORDS

If you keep track of the money coming in and going out, you have totals and a general picture of where you stand, but what about individual documents? My budget might tell me the totals in each category but not the exact amounts for each individual transaction—when and where and how much I paid out or received. Those individual transactions, and proof of them, can be important for checking your records, especially if the Internal Revenue Service audits you.

These days, most people keep track of how their money comes in and goes out on a spreadsheet or some other basic electronic system. They send and receive pertinent documents by email as attachments, usually PDFs, and download and store them in folders on a computer with a couple of clicks.

While more and more financial records are digital, some of us still prefer to keep paper records and receipts. Sometimes we receive them via snail mail. Sometimes we receive them digitally and print them out. For some people, paper receipts are a reassuring backup. If you want to store records on paper, consider acquiring:

- Two large plastic file boxes
- Twelve to 24 hanging file folders

In the first file box, store your tax documentation. In the second box, keep all your other financial documents. It might not seem necessary now, especially if you're just beginning to save your records, but using separate boxes makes it easier to find things when you need them.

I use inexpensive plastic file boxes because they're easy to move and have more than enough room inside. You can find them at any office supply or large all-purpose store. (Hanging file folders are sold anywhere you can find file boxes, but be sure to purchase hanging folders that include labels.)

Try not to make your record-keeping system too elaborate. At the beginning, you're just trying to establish a basic routine. If your methods become too complex, they'll be hard to maintain. Whether electronically or on paper, I recommend that you store the following documents:

- Insurance policies
- Investment paperwork
- Banking documentation
- Credit statements
- Bill stubs

- Paycheck stubs
- Receipts for large or expensive items
- Mortgage papers
- Passports
- Car titles
- Stock certificates
- Annual IRA (individual retirement account) information
- Pension statements

ORGANIZE YOUR RECORDS

Now that you know which records you want to keep, it's time to organize them. Begin by sorting all the financial papers (or electronic files) you believe to be relevant. If you're unsure whether you should save something, save it just in case.

Next, separate your documents into piles (or folders) according to their purpose and organize them chronologically.

Then label the file folders and place them in your file boxes.

Finally, place each pile in the appropriate file folder.

If this system seems ridiculously simple, that's because it is. At this point, you're just starting out, and keeping it simple will eliminate frustration and ensure your success.

Part of organizing your records is determining how long you should keep various documents as well as what can be thrown away. Different people have different opinions on this subject. When you begin the process, you might find the guidelines in the following table helpful. They have worked well for me.

Document	How Long to Keep It
Tax returns and other tax forms	I keep mine indefinitely. Others keep them for seven years because this is how long the IRS is given to perform an audit on any given year. Keep a separate file for each year.
Property records	Keep property records as long as you own the property they pertain to.
Receipts/warranties	This depends on the items purchased. Use your own judgment.
401(k) and IRA statements	I keep my quarterly statements until I receive my annual statement and then shred them. I keep my annual statements indefinitely.
Brokerage statements	I keep these indefinitely for tax purposes.
Mutual fund statements	I keep these indefinitely for tax purposes.
Credit card statements	Keep them for each annual tax file.
Pay stubs	I suggest keeping pay stubs until you receive your W-2 form and then shredding them.
Retirement/savings plan statements	I keep the quarterly statements until I receive the annual statement. I then shred the quarterlies and keep the annual statements indefinitely.
Bank records	Keep them in your annual tax files.
Bills	I shred bills after I have checked the canceled check online. You may consider keeping bills for insured items such as jewelry, appliances, electronics, and collectibles in case you need to file an insurance claim.

I have used this basic system for years. You can use it too or design your own record-keeping system. The main idea is to find a system that works well for you.

BE PATIENT

Remember, there is no single right or wrong way to organize your financial information. Be patient until you find a system that works for you. Developing this record-keeping system will take some time and dedication, but the peace of mind you attain will make it well worth the effort.

CHAPTER 6

MORE BUDGET IDEAS

*P*rivate First Class Allen had just completed basic training when he and his fiancé arrived in our unit. He was assigned to the mortar team in our platoon. It seemed like he was always optimistic, full of energy, and lived for his job. Perhaps you know the type. I was very surprised when he told me how far in debt he was.

He explained to me that three years earlier, when he was 18, he'd been approved for his first credit card. The card had an interest rate of 12% and a $500 credit limit, but that was just the beginning. Three years after graduating from high school, PFC Allen had accumulated nearly $10,000 in debt with five different credit card companies. Not long before we met, in anticipation of his enlistment bonus and the certainty of a steady income from his military pay, he'd financed a brand new vehicle rather than paying down his debt.

PFC Allen and his fiancée now owed nearly $45,000 to lenders and had just found out they were expecting a baby. They were able to make only the minimum payments on their credit cards because of their carefree spending habits. This included the latest electronics, designer clothing, and frequent evenings out in upscale restaurants. There was absolutely nothing left to save at the end of each month. To say the Allens were overwhelmed by their financial situation was an understatement.

This conversation took place over four years ago. Recently, I spoke to Private First Class Allen on the phone and learned that he and his wife had totally turned their finances around. After overhauling their budget and eliminating their frivolous spending habits, they'd been able to pay off all their debt, including their vehicle.

Now they have a new attitude: anything they don't have cash for, they can't afford. Both joined the National Guard and both enrolled in four-year colleges with lucrative careers waiting for them after graduation.

$\sim$

The Allens were fortunate to have the foresight and determination to make these financial changes while they were young. Overcoming their mountain of debt would not have been possible without their willingness to change.

WHEN YOU FIRST JOIN UP

Many new recruits enter the military with a clean financial slate, meaning they have no debt or substantial financial obligations. While completing basic training, the majority of recruits are exempt from common expenses the general public must face, including:

- A home mortgage
- Grocery bills
- Electric bills
- Gas bills
- Cable bills
- Credit card bills
- Automobile payments
- Auto insurance
- Home insurance
- Vehicle and home maintenance

Even after basic training, major expenses such as housing and meals are paid for by the military, leaving new recruits virtually free of major expenses. As we saw in Sergeant Major Austin's case in chapter 1, a great deal of the money that might otherwise go to all these traditional expenses can be routed directly into investments.

TAKE ADVANTAGE OF AUTOMATIC DEDUCTIONS

Automatic electronic deductions from your paycheck into your investment accounts are an investor's best friend. Since the money never enters your pocket, you don't have to worry about not spending it. You don't even miss it, and you have peace of mind knowing that your financial plan is on autopilot.

ALREADY LIVING BELOW YOUR MEANS?

If you're already living below your means, you're that much more ready to retire. Possibly the best part of saving 20% to 30% or more of your current income is that you are already budgeting to live below your means. The day you retire, the level of income you require will be less difficult to replace.

For example, if your salary is $45,000 the day of your retirement and you've been saving 20% of your income, you will need to replace it with $36,000 from your retirement plan instead of the full $45,000. If you live on less than your income long enough, it eventually becomes second nature.

NO TIME LIKE THE PRESENT

Having a difficult time deciding what to do? To begin, start small. You can always increase your savings and investment allotments later. (Information on saving and investing comes in chapters 10 and 11.) Try starting with just 1% of your net income. With time, if you determine the investment has been successful, you can increase the allotment to 2%, then 5%. If you get a reenlistment bonus or raise in pay from earning a higher rank, half of it can be directed straight into your investment plan. Receive a gift or an inheritance? Place half of it in savings before you do anything else. And so on and so forth.

As a brand new military recruit, you might never have a better opportunity to begin securing your financial future. Advantages new recruits enjoy that help them create prosperous financial plans typically include:

- A steady income
- Limited financial obligations
- Benefits provided by the military that promote the ability to save more cash

- Ability to take advantage of investment plans at an extremely young age, allowing assets time to accrue

Most importantly, don't make excuses. Every one of us has things we'd like to spend our paychecks on. But if you're serious about being financially responsible, make saving and investing a priority. Starting your plan today will maximize the compounding effects of your investments. With a lifetime of growth, your early savings could accelerate well beyond the average civilian's.

FROM RAGS TO RICHES

In 2007, United States Marine Corps Private First Class Denise Kennedy had recently completed boot camp training and volunteered to be sent to a unit currently deployed to Iraq. That decision said a great deal about her character.

During downtime, one of PFC Kennedy's favorite topics was asking others how they handled their money. She intended to make the Marine Corps her career and wanted to prepare for a financially healthy retirement afterwards. Kennedy recognized the benefit of planning, budgeting, controlling spending, saving, and investing early, but she didn't know squat about personal finances.

Growing up, her family didn't have money. They were working class people, and pretty much everything they earned went toward their everyday expenses. If they had anything left over, they went to a ball game or camping or bought the kids an extra gift at the holidays.

To begin, PFC Kennedy spent some time online reading about personal finance. Next she created a simple investment plan. It was far from complex. First she established an emergency fund and eliminated credit card debt. Then she contacted an investment company that specialized in working with members of the military and began diverting a portion of her monthly income into the Military Thrift Savings Life Cycle Plan, a Roth IRA, and a mutual stock fund (IRAs and mutual stocks are explained in chapter 11). While deployed, she took advantage of the Military Savings Deposit Program. Ultimately, her plan included:

- A checking account
- A savings account for general funds
- A separate savings account for emergencies
- Three or four CDs in the amount of $1,000
- Use of the military's Savings Deposit Program while on deployment
- Use of the Military Thrift Savings Life Cycle Plan
- A Roth IRA
- A mutual stock index fund

Today, PFC Kennedy considers her financial plan a complete success and is excited about how well her money is working for her. Since she is working with an investment company instead of researching companies on her own, her plan is on autopilot, leaving her with little to worry about.

PFC Kennedy attributes her success to the simplicity of her plan and to taking advantage of the many possibilities for saving and investing, especially those that are offered to military personnel and not the general public. Her patience, foresight, and determination along with the many advantages available to her as a military staffer are paying off. She also attributes her success to having been raised so frugally. She always understood the difference between needs versus wants, something covered in greater detail in the next chapter.

If you share Private First Class Kennedy's interest in investments and you want more information on military investment plans, visit the staff at your military unit's finance department. You'll likely find they're more than willing to help you—and the information is free!

CHAPTER 7

SPEND WISELY:
DIFFERENTIATE
YOUR WANTS
FROM YOUR NEEDS

*U*pon graduating from high school—much to her surprise—
U.S. Army Private Katherine Rayburn received monetary
gifts from friends and family in excess of $17,000. Although
the money was intended to be savings for her future, Private Rayburn
decided she would celebrate her graduation in a number of extravagant ways. Without much thought, she spent the money lavishly on
a variety of luxurious possessions she wanted but didn't really need.
Over the course of the summer, the $17,000 was reduced to under a
thousand dollars in savings.

For educational purposes, let's say Rayburn had spent only $7,000 of the $17,000, leaving $10,000 available to invest conservatively. Let's also say that Rayburn set a goal to retire at the age of 58. This would have left 40 years for the $10,000 to grow with compound interest.

If the $10,000 had been placed in a conventional index fund averaging a 4% annual return, it could have grown to $46,163.66 by the time she retired. If Rayburn had left the fund alone for another 20 years, it could have grown to $101,150.26.

In Rayburn's defense, it's easy to understand her excitement at receiving so much money, but her purchases were based on wants, not needs. Later, with the hard-earned gift of hindsight, she regretted those impulse purchases.

Thanks to her willingness to share her story, it's easy to see how important it is to differentiate wants from needs as well as how saving at an early age can greatly impact long-term savings.

∼

Even after you've thought about your goals and have begun budgeting, you have to take the important step—the lifelong step—of controlling your spending and sticking to your budget.

One of the greatest ways to build wealth, often overlooked and taken for granted, is what I call smart spending. This means getting value for your money, or the biggest bang for your buck. It also means learning how credit cards can be devastating as well as how they can work for you. (I'll say more about credit cards in the next chapter.)

Maybe you're the sort of person who likes to wear expensive designer jeans and has a closetful to prove it. Or maybe you're the sort of person who would rather have one or two nice pairs of jeans that you wear over and over again until they fall apart.

Whatever your profile, you don't need to transform yourself into a skinflint who squeezes every penny and never has any fun today out of fear of being broke tomorrow. But you probably do want to do some planning and adopt some discipline here and there. You want to be able to satisfy the person you are today, the person who wants some cool stuff now like clothes and a car and vacations, while laying the foundation for the person you will become later, the person with enough assets to afford bigger, better, and more important stuff like a house, better cars and vacations, and a comfortable retirement.

Because the spending habits you develop today will have a significant impact on your financial condition in the years to come, it's important to determine what is truly important to you. This means differentiating between your wants and your needs. You can do this now or you can do it in your 40s, 50, or 60s when you're scrambling to save money to make up for the time you've lost, but sooner or later, you'll be forced to do it.

Not surprisingly, you have to determine the difference between your wants and needs before you can successfully create and apply a savings and investment plan.

Hopefully, you agree that now is as good a time as any to do this. As your life evolves, you'll probably realize that the more you can live without, the happier you are, but this can only happen once you've begun to separate your wants from your needs. Let's start with needs.

WHAT ARE NEEDS?

Each of us has certain basic needs that must be met. Examples include:

- Clean water
- Nutrition
- Medical treatment and medication
- Transportation
- A safe place to live
- Clothing

WHAT ARE WANTS?

Once our basic needs are satisfied, we purchase other material items and services. These are wants. They include things that make our lives more enjoyable, comfortable, and convenient but are goods and services we can do without, such as:

- Luxury cars
- Recreational vehicles such as boats, snowmobiles, and motorcycles
- Second homes
- Home computers
- A laundering service
- High-speed internet
- Jewelry
- New furniture
- Swimming pools
- Premium TV packages

- Entertainment such as going to movies or concerts
- Eating out
- Designer clothing

Notice how the list of wants could go on and on and on? Many of us probably spend more than we can afford to on luxury items and services we could actually do without.

EVERYONE'S NEEDS AND WANTS ARE DIFFERENT

One individual's wants may be another person's needs and vice versa. For example, a farmer might *need* a four wheel-drive diesel truck to operate on his farm. On the contrary, a teenager in a large city might *want* the same type of vehicle but might not necessarily *need* it. In fact, it is certainly much more economical to own a smaller vehicle in a large city.

NEEDS CHANGE

Throughout our lives, our needs continuously change. From the time we are infants to the time we retire, the things we need evolve. Factors that alter our needs include:

- Marriage
- A death in the family
- Having children
- Divorce
- A sudden injury
- Health concerns

NEEDS CAN BE PERCEIVED RATHER THAN REAL

Modern society has created a multitude of new goods and services that many people view as needs. Examples include:

- Fuel-consuming SUVs
- Cell phones
- Eight-dollar cups of coffee
- Cable TV with 1,300 channels
- Designer clothes
- Computer games

These are just a few of the luxuries many people consider to be modern-day staples. Marketing and advertising campaigns lead us to believe we can't live life to the fullest without them. As a result, living beyond our means has become a common theme that our supersizing culture promotes and fuels by addiction to credit cards.

DETERMINE YOUR WANTS AND NEEDS

Every time you find yourself about to purchase something, stop and consider whether it's a want or a need. Simultaneously, begin keeping a record of what you spend over the course of one month. Then compare what you spend to your monthly income. This will show you exactly how much money you spend on things you want but don't necessarily need. Continue to do this for several months.

Over time, you will likely notice a significant decrease in your spending. Either way, you will be able to see exactly where your money is going and where you can make appropriate adjustments.

A record of your spending matched against your budget will provide a visual representation of your cash flow, making it much easier to monitor. Once you begin to get organized, you'll be well on your way to living a less expensive and more fulfilling life!

The following table offers a relatively simple example of spending matched against a budget:

Income	Proposed	Actual	% of income
Military pay	$1,000.00	$1,081.32	
Other income	$0.00	$0.00	
Total Income	**$1,000.00**	**$1,081.32**	
Fixed Expenses			
Cell phone	$50.00	$48.92	5%
Credit card	$60.00	$58.50	6%
Auto insurance	$90.00	$89.66	9%
Internet	$60.00	$59.99	6%
Total Fixed Expenses	**$260.00**	**$257.07**	**26%**
Variable Expenses			
Food/personal	$150.00	$149.45	15%
Gas	$50.00	$48.41	5%
Entertainment	$65.00	$64.67	7%
Utilities	$75.00	$73.18	7%
Total Variable Expenses	**$340.00**	**$335.71**	**34%**
Total Expenses	**$600.00**	**$592.78**	**60%**
$ Remaining in Budget	**$400.00**	**$408.76**	**40%**

You can use many strategies and techniques to structure your budget and determine how much money you have to spend. Two simple and time-proven favorites follow.

UTILIZE THE 50/30/20 BUDGET CONCEPT

The 50/30/20 budget is based on the concept of needs and wants. The fact that new recruits are exempt from many common expenses makes this budget very feasible for military service people. Here's how it works.

50%—Must Haves

Fifty percent of your spending is designated for "must haves" such as food, gas, vehicle insurance, etc. In other words, your goal is to limit your "must haves" to 50% of your after-tax income.

30%—Wants

Thirty percent of your spending is designated for "wants." Your "wants" are allowed to take up 30% of your after-tax income.

20%—Savings

Twenty percent of your spending is designated for "savings." This remaining 20% of your budget is automatically directed into your savings and investment plan.

Simplified, your target savings and investment goal is 20% of your net (after taxes) income. The 20% savings with this plan can be split in half, with 10% placed in a regular savings account and the remaining 10% automatically directed into a conservative investment such as the military's Thrift Savings Plan (TSP). When your regular savings reach a benchmark amount, invest all but $1,000 in a mutual fund or similar instrument and begin building it again.

This is a simple plan, and it's absolutely effective.

UTILIZE THE 60% SOLUTION

With this technique, you use percentages to determine your monthly spending. Ideally, 60% of your income is set aside for monthly expenses, hence the name. These are often the items that cause a budget to fail because most people don't budget for them. The other 40% is divided among your retirement account, short- and long-term savings, and entertainment.

To begin, multiply the amount of your monthly income, say $4,000, by 60%, or 0.60. $4,000 times 0.6 = $2,400. This is the amount you should spend on things like housing, vehicle expenses, the internet, cable, food, utilities, and other monthly bills.

Now subtract this amount from the total. The remaining amount can be divided evenly or however else you choose to divide it among your retirement account, emergency fund or debt reduction, short-term savings for periodic expenses, and entertainment.

Let's look a closer look at how this budget strategy works. Keep in mind that your percentages will vary, and some of the expenses might not even apply if you are currently serving in the military.

60% Monthly Expenses

This includes items such as housing, food, utilities, vehicles, insurance, and child care. These are typically the costs of living that are most frequently considered when establishing a budget.

10% Short-Term Savings

This short-term savings account is designated for periodic expenses. Examples include medical expenses, vehicle maintenance or repairs (not including insurance premiums), appliances, home maintenance, and holiday and birthday gifts. This account gives you confidence that you will have the money for these expenses as they arise and that you will not overspend beyond your planned budget.

10% Long-Term Savings or Debt Reduction

If you are in debt (not including a home mortgage), it might be wise to use this portion of the budget to pay off your debts. You can even draw some from the other categories, such as retirement, to increase this to about 20% for now. After your debt has been paid off, it might be wise to consult a financial advisor regarding a conservative approach to investing these funds since they are intended for long-term savings. An example could be an index fund due to its liquidity and relatively low risk.

10% Retirement

When establishing retirement funds, strongly consider having these accounts set up for automatic withdrawal. To begin, this money could be invested in the military's Thrift Savings Plan (TSP) or a Roth IRA.

10% Entertainment

Service members perform some of the most difficult jobs in the world and spend long hours each day doing them. These funds should be set aside for you to enjoy!

STAY FLEXIBLE

In the military, fragmentary orders are abbreviated operations orders that are used to adjust or modify the original order. They eliminate the need to restate information and create a whole new order. You can apply this same approach to your budget. From month to month, your lifestyle might change without notice. If so, you can adjust your finances along the way.

Marriage or divorce, newborn babies, deployment orders, unexpected illnesses, and physical injuries can require you to adjust your finances. If you have set up a budget that addresses unexpected costs, you can simply adjust the numbers as needed. Your planning and flexibility ensure your financial stability.

MAINTAIN YOUR PLAN
ON A WEEKLY BASIS

Your budget will need routine maintenance to ensure its accuracy. As mentioned earlier, you should devote 15 to 20 minutes a week to reviewing your budget and confirming that your finances are in order. Set aside a day and time when you take a look at your finances each week. This routine will provide you with the peace of mind that you're not overextending yourself by spending too much.

BEWARE THE TIMES YOU LIVE IN

It's easy to lose perspective when it looks like everyone around you has it all. The fact is, no one has it all, but we live in a society that wants us to think other people do. If that happens, we're more likely to confuse our wants with our needs and start overspending.

The "I Want It Now" Society

I hear many people say that today's generation attempts to have everything their parents have at an age when they can't afford it. In a society where credit is routinely available, who is responsible? Is it the borrower or the lender?

Many borrowers undoubtedly use poor judgment. However, in their defense, the temptation is to say yes when lenders don't require a single penny for a down payment on a new home available with a balloon loan. For some, such offers are too enticing to resist. The same goes when vehicles that are well beyond a borrower's means can be financed for up to seven years. Or when countless luxury items are available for purchase with the simple swipe of a credit card.

But borrowers have to remember that, until these items are paid for, they don't own them. In the meantime, credit card and loan companies charge outrageous monthly interest rates. Understanding this is the borrowers' responsibility.

The "I Work Hard—I Deserve a Reward!" Mentality

Men and women from all walks of life often feel they deserve to be rewarded for their hard work. For generations, servicemen and servicewomen have rewarded themselves with all sorts of extravagant material items upon returning home from deployment to a war zone. With modern combat pay increases and sizable reenlistment bonuses, luxurious rewards for hard work have never been more enticing.

Planning to spend a modest portion of your earnings on luxury items upon return from deployment can be a source of motivation while overseas. However, spending every cent you have saved can suddenly turn from a motivator into a financial nightmare. One solution is to focus some of your attention on nontangible rewards such as:

- The peace of mind you get from having zero debt
- An investment portfolio building wealth for you
- A clear vision of your financially secure future
- The ability to pay a sizable amount of cash toward a new home
- Retirement at an earlier age than you might otherwise be able to afford

A simpler lifestyle can benefit you in a number of ways. The confidence you gain from living a financially sound and secure life will help you develop a sense of pride that will last long after any luxury item has diminished in value. You might find your peers admiring the confidence you exude thanks to your debt-free lifestyle, but mainly you will experience a deeper sense of happiness when you realize you are getting by without all the expensive things you can't really afford anyway.

Why not consider giving a simpler lifestyle a try? You can always spend the money later if you decide the simple life isn't for you. What do you have to lose?

CELEBRATE INTANGIBLE BENEFITS

Often, military personnel who deploy to developing nations and war zones acquire nontangible assets that prove to be more valuable than any monetary gain.

Perspective on Material Items

In addition to appreciating the things they already have, service members deployed in war zones often gain an enhanced understanding of the material possessions they can do without. This elevated level of gratitude can dramatically alter their perspective on life and is nearly unavoidable after returning home from a developing nation besieged by war and plagued by poverty and disease.

Appreciation of Health

Dismal images of innocent people struggling to survive not only change people's point of view toward luxurious material items they once considered essential but also help them place a superior value on the basics of life such as good health, clean water, food, clothing, and a safe neighborhood to live in.

After seeing those who are unable to attain these basic requirements, the objects they once desired begin to seem insignificant. This feeling is compounded when they realize their health could be taken from them at any time. In addition, after witnessing unimaginable levels of suffering, many who serve in the armed forces develop a deeper sense of gratitude for their own health and the well-being of those they love.

Gratitude for Freedom

Following a deployment to a developing nation, military personnel usually gain a fuller understanding of what it means to live in a country free of tyranny and based on freedom and civil liberties. After experiencing the conditions of good people who are far less fortunate, it is common to develop a heightened level of appreciation for the blessing of being born in such a privileged nation.

PICK YOUR POISON

Would you rather pay your dues now or in your golden years? As far as motivation goes, you might try considering the financial sacrifices you make today as a way of "paying your dues" for a promising financial future tomorrow. At one point or another, we all have to pay our dues. Why not do it now, while you're young and healthy? It's easier to get by with less today than it will be later in life. Once you begin moving toward a financially secure future, your motivation will increase because you will have a prosperous future to look forward to.

If you choose to pay your dues now by not spending your money on unnecessary material items or services that only make your life more convenient, your portfolio has the potential to grow at a tremendously greater rate. If you choose to pay your dues later by spending unnecessarily today, you will work harder for less money during the years when you could be enjoying life the most.

GOOD NEWS FOR THE NEXT GENERATION

My hope is that future generations will be taught more conservative spending habits and that individuals will learn lessons about the pitfalls of accumulating debt by observing the spending habits of today's consumers. Should this happen, young people will not only benefit financially but also will discover that true satisfaction in life comes from faith, family, friendship, and helping others.

CHAPTER 8

PAY CASH
TO SAVE CASH

S taff Sergeant Anderson, United States Air Force, has a winning strategy for sticking to his budget: "We pay cash for everything we purchase. It's that simple."

Then he admitted that he had his wife to thank for this winning strategy. Before becoming engaged, he'd made many of the typical impulse purchases young people make when they first begin receiving a paycheck.

His first major investment after his enlistment was a brand new truck and then a brand new all-terrain vehicle shortly thereafter. In order to get the vehicles, he financed almost the entire cost of both. After paying his monthly obligations to the lenders and insurance, his checking account often fell below the minimum amount and was *charged an additional fee. Then he got married. Thankfully, his bride took charge of the household finances.*

"Becoming a cash-only person brought a feeling of empowerment," Staff Sergeant Anderson stated. *"Every pay period, I make a withdrawal from an ATM for enough cash to last me the next two weeks. With cash, I don't need to worry about overspending or tracking how much is left. I use the cash to pay for gas, groceries, and entertainment. Entertainment can be anything such as books, movies, fishing tackle, etc. By withdrawing these cash allotments twice a month, I know at a glance how much I have left until payday. This system virtually eliminates the need to use a debit or credit card. Also, I can roll any cash left over from one pay period to the next. Sometimes it isn't even necessary to withdraw the full amount allotted from the ATM. This system is extremely gratifying,"* he concluded. *"Give it a try!"*

~

After their marriage, the Andersons realized that if they didn't make serious changes to their spending habits, they would be in debt for years to come. Together, they decided to set distinct goals. To expedite the process, they sold Mrs. Anderson's vehicle, which she fully owned, for cash. They used the cash from the sale to pay down debt. Then they reestablished their budget to pay off the other vehicles and two major credit cards over the next two years. After making the necessary sacrifices to accomplish their mission, they decided they would never again use anything but cash for their expenditures, including vehicles.

Like Staff Sergeant Anderson, you too could try using cash and eliminating debit and credit cards. It can make a life-changing difference in your ability to save.

MONEY-SAVING TIPS

General money-saving tips that work well include:

- Bringing lunches, snacks, and beverages to work
- Making coffee at home rather than visiting the local coffee shop
- Renting movies to watch at home rather than going to the theater
- Quitting smoking (This will improve your health too!)
- Paying with cash, not credit
- Buying used through the use of classified ads in the paper, looking online, shopping at used retail shops, and going to garage sales
- Reading more books checked out for free at the library
- Assessing old collections and selling off those you've lost interest in, everything from stamp collections to baseball card collections
- Limiting the amount you spend for birthdays and drawing names for the holidays
- Giving yourself a haircut; the military haircut is the easiest!
- Sealing your home, assuming you own one, to prevent drafts, which saves heating and cooling costs

To save money on vehicles:

- Never buy new

- Shop online for quality preowned vehicles
- Keep driving your old car if it still works reliably
- Pay cash for your vehicles
- Properly inflate your tires to decrease fuel consumption
- Slow down when driving to decrease fuel consumption
- Maintain your automobile to save on repairs as well as to decrease fuel consumption

To save money on banking:

- Use automatic bill pay to reduce rates and fees and save money on postage and checks (It's good for the environment too!)
- Pay with cash; issue yourself an allotment of cash rather than using debit or ATM cards, which sometimes charge fees.
- Avoid banks with excessive fees; shop around for accounts with low or no fees

To save money on credit cards:

- Consider cancelling them; you'll save money by purchasing fewer items and not paying interest
- Ask for a rate reduction for any credit cards you keep; if you reliably pay your bills on time and threaten to drop the cards if you can't have a lower rate, companies might agree to the reduction

- Never carry your credit card in your wallet; this requires you to think about the purchase before you use it
- Consolidate your credit card debt; this can lower your interest rate and the time it takes to pay off your debt

To save money on food:

- Make a shopping list and stick to it; this will help you avoid unplanned and unnecessary purchases
- Eat at the chow hall and use the PX's grocery store flyer to plan meals based on items that are on sale
- Use coupons, especially on sale items, to save even more
- Avoid grocery shopping when you're hungry
- Stock up on staple items when they're on sale
- Pack a cooler for long drives or day trips; this is cheaper than eating out
- Cook with a slow cooker; these meals often combine readily available and low-cost foods
- Make casseroles when ingredients are on sale and freeze them to eat when you don't have time to cook; you will save twice, first by purchasing sale items and second by eliminating the need to eat out
- Cook with generic products; the quality of generics and store brands is often identical to name brands, and the price is much more affordable

CUT UP YOUR CREDIT CARDS

Credit cards typically charge high interest rates and promote overspending. Because it's so easy to use them, people seldom think carefully about their purchases. Unless you can pay off your balance each and every month so that you don't pay interest, consider cutting up your cards or limiting them to emergency use only. Purchases on credit cards are often for smaller items. If you can't pay cash for the smaller item, why use a credit card to buy it? You obviously can't afford the item!

If you must have a credit card, leave it at home in a safe location and bring it with you only when you absolutely need it—while traveling, for example.

USE AUTOMATIC BILL PAY

I set up electronic automatic withdrawals so that my bills are automatically paid from my checking account. This gives me peace of mind, lets me avoid writing and mailing checks each month, and saves on stamps and envelopes. Examples of bills that can be paid automatically include:

- Utilities
- Rent
- Mortgage
- Cell phone
- Internet
- Auto loan

USE THE ENVELOPE SYSTEM

This old-fashioned budgeting system has been around a long time and is based on using cash to pay for the majority of goods and services rather than a debit or credit card. It might be too Jurassic for you, but, then again, it might be just what you need to get you to stick to your budget.

Even if you don't use actual envelopes or exclusively use cash, the principles are the same. The system is simple and it works, especially for those who have a tendency to use credit cards to make impulse purchases without giving the cost a second thought. To create an effective envelope system, follow the four steps below.

1. Budget each paycheck. A tight budget is a must if you're going to successfully implement this system, so work out your budget and determine the amount of money required to pay your monthly bills. The more accurate you are, the more effective your envelope system will be.

2. Decide how much money from each paycheck to deposit into savings.

3. Decide how much to allow from each paycheck into your other predetermined categories. These are areas where overspending might occur if there were no control mechanism. I use four envelopes, one each for groceries, clothing, gas, and entertainment. For example, I allot money this way:

   - $200 for groceries
   - $100 for clothing

- $75 for gas
- $50 for entertainment

4. Place the predetermined amount of cash in each envelope and use it for the designated expense. For example, if you allow $50 for entertainment, put $50 cash in your entertainment envelope for the pay period.

That's it! When the envelope is empty, you're done spending for that pay period.

If you have extra money in any of the envelopes at the end of the month, you can add it to the amount you get to spend the following month. Or you can remove it from the envelope and put it into savings. That's it. Simple and effective.

Be aware that if you have an expensive night on the town and spend your entire $50 on entertainment in one evening, you must discipline yourself not to spend any more on entertainment until your next pay period, when you can budget for that category again.

Hold yourself accountable. *No cheating allowed!* This system takes discipline and time to get used to. Do your best not to simply visit an ATM when you find yourself short on cash in any particular category. Remember, you can always reassess your budget each month and adjust your predetermined allotment ahead of time.

Even though the funds used with your debit card come directly from your checking or savings account, the ease of use causes many to overspend. Since paying with cash is more difficult than swiping plastic, becoming a cash-only consumer makes it less likely you'll overspend or buy on impulse.

Finally, be patient. Establishing a responsible spending plan is part of your lifestyle, not a passing experiment. Your financial routines might take months or years to perfect. Don't give up after a month or two if you become frustrated. Eventually you'll like knowing where and how much you're spending each pay period. Trust me—staying financially stable is something you'll be proud of. If you're patient, you'll see for yourself how exciting it can be to live a debt-free lifestyle and build wealth!

As I mentioned, how you organize your spending will likely evolve, but no matter what you try, you will quickly gain confidence from knowing you're taking charge of your financial future.

AVOID IMPULSE PURCHASES

Remember Staff Sergeant Anderson at the start of this chapter with his brand new truck and all-terrain vehicle? Thanks to his new bride, he was able to recover from his impulse purchases, but not everyone is so lucky.

Uninformed decisions and the powerful enticement of today's luxuries and conveniences affect the judgment of many serving in the military, especially when transactions for new vehicles can be completed with 100% financing, no cash down.

Though it took an unscrupulous salesperson as well as a lending institution with liberal guidelines to complete these transactions, Staff Sergeant Anderson made the final decision to live beyond his means.

We cannot depend on other people to do what is best for us, especially people who are trying to sell us something. We need to think before we jump and do our best to avoid making impulse purchases.

CHAPTER 9

GET OUT OF DEBT,
STAY OUT OF DEBT

*I*n 2011, Air Force Master Sergeant William Jacobson had just returned from his first deployment to Afghanistan in support of Operation Enduring Freedom. During his deployment, he and his wife, Theresa, managed to save a great deal of his combat pay. Oddly enough, they accumulated a great deal of credit card debt at the same time.

"I know that sounds ridiculous," he told me years later. "Why didn't we just pay cash rather than use credit cards for everyday goods and services? I was earning more money than ever, but we were still charging purchases on credit cards due to old habits and what we perceived as convenience."

The Jacobsons' wake-up call was a late payment for the third month in a row on one of their numerous credit cards. The late fee seemed unreasonably high, and it triggered the couple to study the details of their credit card bills. To their dismay, they learned they were paying 20% annual interest in addition to late fees. They wouldn't buy something knowing they would pay 20% more for it, so why were they doing it with credit cards?

The Jacobsons' only excuse was that they were disorganized and had no established routine to pay bills on time. "This initiated our decision to get a fresh start financially," the master sergeant recalls. "We were determined to get out of debt and stay out of debt."

~

If this chapter about debt doesn't apply to you, congratulations! With no debt to pay off, you are well ahead of the average American citizen in regard to saving for your future. To state the obvious, having no debt to pay is an enormous advantage and will allow you to accelerate your savings and investment plans.

However, if you're like the majority of Americans, you probably owe some type of financial obligation. Perhaps you have high credit card bills. Perhaps you're paying on student loans. Perhaps vehicle loans leave you strapped each month. If you're struggling to meet your monthly expenses or find yourself paying monthly bills with your credit card, you might be experiencing serious financial problems that could even result in bankruptcy.

Getting out of debt can be challenging, especially if you're paying excessive interest rates and fees, but it doesn't have to be this way.

ELIMINATE DEBT FIRST

Mathematically, it doesn't make sense to deposit $5,000 in a mutual fund anticipating a 4% return if you owe $10,000 in credit card debt with a 12% interest rate. Thus, before you begin developing a serious investment plan, eliminate all of your debt with the exception of a home mortgage. Becoming debt free should be your primary goal. In other words, when you begin investing, do so with a clean slate. This strategy makes mathematical sense, and you will develop a new respect for good spending habits once you see how difficult it can be to pay off the debts you currently owe.

A Mathematical Example

The table below reveals the astronomical sum of money you can save by paying off your credit cards as quickly as possible. Assume that the owners of this card have stopped using it and are merely paying off debt they have already accumulated.

Credit Card Debt	Monthly Payment	Interest Rate	Months to Pay Off Debt	Estimated Total Interest Accrued
$20,000.00	$264.30	10%	120	$11,716.18
$20,000.00	$424.94	10%	60	$5,496.45
Savings				$6,219.73

By choosing to pay off credit card debt in five years rather than 10, they can save more than $6,000! On the other hand, those who pay only the minimum amount they owe on a credit card each month can wind up paying more in interest than the cost of the original purchase!

If you increase your monthly payment by even the slightest amount, you dramatically cut the time it takes to pay off your debt in addition to the total interest you pay. As you can see, purchasing a little less and reducing your debt a little more can make a tremendous difference.

DEVELOP A PLAN FOR PAYING OFF DEBT

Once you've determined how much of your monthly budget to use to pay off debt, form a strategy. This is not an exact science. Some individuals prefer to set a goal of paying off the credit card with the highest interest rate first. Others pay off debts with the smallest balances first to simplify their monthly obligations and see fast results. Additional techniques are presented below. Explore different methods, find what works best for you, and stick with it.

Consolidate Debt

If you owe money to more than one credit card company, you might want to consolidate your debt. This technique consists of transferring the balance on high interest cards to lower interest cards and then canceling the card or cards with high interest rates. It can save you money in interest and the labor of paying so many bills per month, which lessens the possibility of missed payments and late fees, but use extreme caution. Sometimes companies hide transfer fees and penalties in their company guidelines. It is important to remember that these companies make money by offering you low monthly payments. They might not perceive paying off your credit balance as a good thing and might even penalize you for doing so.

Employ the Snowball Effect

The snowball effect can be a tremendous motivator when it comes to paying off debt on more than one credit card. This strategy is based on the fact that while you are paying extra on one credit card, you must still make the minimum payments on the others. Once you finish paying off a given card, simply apply the amount you were paying on it each month to another credit card in addition to the minimum payment you were making. Each debt you pay off will take less time than the last.

Accelerate Your Debt Payment

Are you anticipating a sizable tax refund or reenlistment bonus? These can be excellent accelerators in debt reduction if you plan ahead. Simply use the money to blast away credit card debt or a car loan. Plan ahead, earmark the additional funds in advance, and then pretend you never received them. Chances are you won't even miss the extra income. You will gain the money back in short order through the interest you won't have to pay.

Stay Out of Debt by Using Cash

Here's a not-so-original thought provided you've read chapter 7— pay cash to save cash. With the possible exception of your home, if you can't pay cash for a purchase, you can't afford it! This simple concept requires nothing but discipline and patience. Save up your money while earning interest on it—and then buy with cash!

Purchase Your Next Vehicle with Cash

Contrary to popular belief, people do still pay cash for vehicles. What's more, they find it extremely gratifying. Start small. If you shop around, you can find plenty of reliable vehicles for sale by their owners at affordable prices. After purchasing a reliable vehicle with cash, you can continue to save to upgrade your vehicle in the future—again with cash.

When you find a vehicle you can afford that appears to be clean and mechanically sound, offer less than the asking price and pay with cash. That's it. Car salespeople like cash sales and are often happy to give a discount for a quick, easy sale. You will save on your monthly insurance bill and avoid a monthly payment to boot.

Over the years, you can upgrade in make and model with your accumulated savings. After you upgrade your vehicle, you can sell the old one and deposit that money back into your savings plan. By starting small and paying cash, you can avoid outrageous interest rates, dealership costs, and sales fees. In the long term, you'll enjoy lower insurance rates as well.

Don't Use Your Emergency Account to Pay Off Debt

The next chapter discusses how and why to establish an emergency account. For now, let me just caution you against using this account to pay down debt. Paying off debt as soon as possible is extremely important, but don't use your emergency account to do so.

The purpose of the emergency account is to cover your expenses if and when emergencies arise. If you exhaust this vital resource, you could end up further in debt if you're forced to use credit to handle true unexpected emergencies. Pretend the emergency fund doesn't even exist unless you're facing a real emergency.

Avoid Using Your Credit Card

Credit cards are the elephant in the room, but if you're still tempted to whip out your plastic, here are 10 reasons not to:

1. The average consumer spends more with credit cards than with cash.
2. Using credit cards increases the risk of identity theft.
3. Credit cards can cause consumers to fall behind on monthly bills.
4. Tracking and paying credit card bills is more work than paying with cash.
5. Credit card companies generally charge a higher interest rate than conventional lenders.
6. Credit cards subject consumers to outlandish penalties and fees.
7. Rewards promoted by credit card lenders only entice consumers to use their cards more.
8. Credit cards can increase the tendency to make impulse purchases.
9. Credit cards simply create another monthly bill a person is responsible for paying.
10. Overextending credit can exacerbate a financial recession.

If you're smart, this list should convince you that overusing credit cards for daily spending is a bad idea. Wise up. Cancel your credit cards and cut them up today.

You will be glad you did tomorrow!

Avoid Those Impulse Purchases!

Again, impulse buying occurs when you get caught up in the excitement of a situation and purchase something without giving it enough consideration. Usually, this means buying something you don't really need or even want. Sale signs stating "50% off today only!" are retailers' attempts to provoke impulse buying. To prevent yourself from giving in to such temptations, slow down and take time to consider the purchase.

I avoid impulsive purchases by walking away from the item in question and giving it time. For larger ticket items, I give myself a month to think about it. If I still feel like I need the item after that, I'm probably right.

A credit card plus a person with impulsive tendencies is a volatile combination. Purchasing items you don't need with money you don't have is a disaster right from the beginning. These spending practices can propel you into a financial scenario that can end in bankruptcy.

Save up and pay cash. You might even find that by the time you save the money for something, you don't want or need the item anymore. Many people find it more difficult to hand over cash than to swipe a credit card. Remember, if you don't have cash for something, you can't afford it.

Don't Try to Keep up with the Joneses

Professional athletes, rock stars, and TV celebrities making millions escalate the desire to "Keep up with the Joneses" by flaunting their flamboyant, wasteful behavior in the faces of the working class. Is it possible this affects how young people spend their money?

Absolutely. Many try to emulate these lifestyles without fully understanding the true cost. While doing so, they often max out numerous sources of credit.

When creating your own financial plan, consider a comfortable but conservative lifestyle. Be realistic. Set quality long-term goals for your future rather than raising the bar too high just to keep up with the modern-day Joneses.

Never Give Up

If you're struggling with your finances and debt reduction, look online for financial advice blogs. You will quickly realize that countless other people struggle with the same concerns. By interacting with people whose stories are similar to your own, you might come across some additional ideas that will work for you.

Just Do It!

The bottom line is, you need to make a plan to reduce your debt. A good plan today is better than a perfect plan tomorrow. And no matter how you do it, becoming debt free will have the same result: a secure future free of financial anxiety.

DEBT IN REVIEW

To avoid debt:

- Cut up your credit cards. Use cash for all your purchases and don't take on any debt with the exception of purchasing a home. If you must have a credit card, set the limit low and keep the card at home.

- Observe spending tendencies and place limits on them.

- If you want or need something, save up the money and purchase it with cash. By the time you've saved up the money, you might decide you don't need the item anymore.

- Make a plan, also called a budget. Any plan is better than no plan.

- Plan your budget using an electronic spreadsheet or program. By tracking your expenses electronically, you will be able to see at a glance how much you spend in each category and can easily spot your problem areas.

- Each month, set your budget so that you spend less than you earn. A structured budget is the key to avoiding overspending and the unaccountable use of credit.

- Be aware of upcoming expenses and plan for them accordingly so you don't have to use any type of credit when they come due.

- Contribute the maximum amount to your 401(k) if you have one. If you don't have one, look into how you could establish one.

- Each time your cost-of-living allowance (COLA) increases or you get promoted in rank, increase your 401(k) contribution by 1% to 2%. If you don't ever see the money, how can you miss it?

- Be creative in how you entertain yourself and your family. Soon you'll discover ways to do this without spending a penny. Go to free events and spend time with friends.

- Cook your own meals. Avoid eating out except on very special occasions.

- Start a garden. Some military bases have community gardens. With a small plot of ground, you can grow tomatoes, peas, beans, and even herbs. No garden? You can grow a ton of vegetables in containers right on your back porch. Gardening is inexpensive, healthy, and fun!

- Keep an open mind while searching for tools that work for you. If the tools aren't working, keep searching and discover new tools.

- You can find countless personal budgeting ideas on the internet. Talk to friends and family about what works for them and talk to professional advisors to see how they can help.

To get out of debt:

- Build up an emergency fund first and pay off debt second.
- Stop using credit cards to make it to the next paycheck and celebrate cutting them up.
- Don't overpay your debts. Follow your budget so you have enough money left for routine expenses.
- Be patient.
- Use the snowball effect to organize debt elimination.
- Get your momentum going by attacking the smallest balance of debt with all the extra cash you have available, then moving on to the next lowest balance of debt.
- Pay off sources of debt with the highest interest rates first.
- Set realistic goals.
- If you began accumulating debt four or five years ago, recognize that it might take time to eliminate your debt.
- Stop spending!
- You might not see immediate results with your new plan, but in time you will succeed.
- Stop borrowing money. Period.
- Completely eliminate the use of car loans, cash advances, home equity loans, etc. If you can't afford to make a purchase with cash, you can't afford it!

- Plan ahead of time to commit anticipated bonuses and pay raises to eliminating debt or put these in your long-term savings plan.
- For motivation, track your debt reduction on a spreadsheet. The data will indicate the effectiveness of your plan as well as provide a time frame for getting completely out of debt.

To spread good financial hygiene:

- Communicate openly with your spouse regarding your finances to avoid competing interests but be aware that the only person you can control is yourself.
- If your spouse is partly the cause of your financial debt, try leading by example. When your savings account begins to reflect your efforts to begin changing your spending habits, your spouse might be excited to follow your example.
- Develop good habits to use as examples for your children.
- Be willing to make sacrifices. Put a note in your wallet asking, "Is this a need or a want?" Routinely examine your needs versus your wants.
- For inspiration, subtract the cost of "wants" from your monthly budget and multiply the amount by 12. The annual summation of "wants" will expose the amount of money you will have in your savings account at the end of the year. This simple exercise

convinces many to feel differently about the expense of the "wants" in question.

- Review your financial spreadsheet every month, sometimes with family members, to help them understand modern family finances.

- Envision your future and talk about it with your spouse and maybe your children if appropriate. Stay focused on where you will be five, 10, or 15 years from now. These dates will be here sooner than you think.

- Routinely educate others in your unit so that they too can choose to avoid costly financial pitfalls throughout their careers.

THE JACOBSONS TODAY

When Master Sergeant Jacobson and his wife finally tackled their financial mess, they started by completing the following;

1. established a $2,000 cash emergency fund paid off their credit cards, eliminating high interest rates and potential late fees that had been draining their pockets

2. moved out of married housing and became home owners, building equity with their home as a cornerstone investment

3. engaged with a financial planner and created a financial portfolio for retirement, including financial tools provided by the military and other recommended investments

The Jacobsons are now on sound financial footing, both today and in the long term.

"During a second deployment to Afghanistan in 2013," the master sergeant recalls, "we realized the opportunity we had. We were well aware that our savings would accelerate tremendously from the increased income from combat pay. Although we were anxious about me being in harm's way, we were excited to pay off all our credit card bills and our auto loan to finally become debt free. We also signed up for the military's Savings Deposit Program (SDP). This is a wonderful, safe, convenient program that at the time earned 10% interest. By the time I completed my second tour, we had accumulated a six-month emergency fund and organized a well-planned investment portfolio with the assistance of a responsible financial planner."

Looking back, Master Sergeant Jacobson says, "Those ridiculous late fees were a blessing in disguise since they convinced us to finally make serious financial changes."

CHAPTER 10

SAVING AND INVESTING: FIRST STEPS

*A*fter he enlisted, Staff Sergeant Harold Fritz spent every cent of his hard-earned pay. That's what money is for, right? He didn't save anything.

After completing his first year in the military, he realized he had nothing to show for his time and effort, so he decided to make a change and start saving a portion of his pay. He wasn't sure where to begin, so he simply began saving $10 every day. He stuck with this for his remaining three years in the service.

Before long, Staff Sergeant Fritz realized the money he was saving could add up to $50,000 by age 65, maybe more, depending *on interest rates. This was without adding an additional cent to the roughly $11,000 he had saved by putting away $10 a day over his last three years in the service.*

Sergeant Fritz did some more reckoning. If he kept saving $10 a day every day from age 25 to age 65, and if interest rates averaged 2% (a good rate by 2019 standards but low by the long-range averages over recent decades), he'd end up with more than $200,000 in the bank when he retired.

~

How is it possible to save such a vast sum of money on $10 a day?

Designing a lifelong structured investment plan can seem overwhelming. For many, the most difficult part is getting started, but once you've mastered the basics, you will discover that an effective investment portfolio isn't so challenging after all. It's merely a matter of simple arithmetic.

A basic interest-paying savings account at the local bank, credit union, or savings and loan is a great place to start. Although it might seem simple, this account lays the foundation for your successful financial plan. A savings account can help you manage your financial goals and earn interest at the same time, helping your savings grow.

As discussed earlier, interest payments are "passive" income, money that comes in automatically without you rolling up your sleeves and earning it hour by hour. Passive income via investments is how rich people get richer. Instead of working for their money, their money works for them. A savings account is a convenient place to store your money that helps you use cash instead of credit, and it helps you meet your goals sooner than if you saved your money in a lock box or under the mattress.

START EARLY

The best time to start saving money is yesterday. The second best time is today. The next best time is tomorrow. Maybe you're one of those natural savers, someone who's been squirreling away money since childhood, but most of us aren't, and we have to learn how to be.

Look for a financial institution that makes it easy to open and make deposits to a savings account. It might be convenient to have a checking account linked to the savings account so that it's easier to move money back and forth as needed.

Ask questions before you open an account. How much are fees? Are fees lower (zero is best) somewhere else? Does the institution allow your paycheck to be automatically deposited? That's an awfully easy way to make sure your deposits are made since the money goes from your paycheck to the bank automatically, without the time and trouble—and temptation—of you needing to make the deposit yourself.

Look for a savings account that is Federal Deposit Insurance Corporation (FDIC) insured; the FDIC is a federal agency that insures deposits in member banks up to $250,000. If the bank goes broke or is defrauded, you get your money back.

Those who serve in the military have an enormous advantage over their civilian counterparts if they begin saving immediately. While others haven't even begun to think about a savings plan, military personnel can be well on their way to securing their financial future, and they typically need to make fewer financial adjustments in their lifestyles down the road.

SELECT YOUR BANK AND OPEN YOUR FIRST SAVINGS ACCOUNT

Following the steps below will help you open your first savings account as smoothly and inexpensively as possible.

1. Confirm the accessibility of deposits. Every bank has its own guidelines for depositing and withdrawing funds. If you intend to use an ATM regularly, find out what fees are associated with the process. If there are no fees associated with using the ATM at your bank, avoid ATMs at other banks that will charge you $2 or $3 each time you withdraw cash.

2. Check for monthly maintenance fees. Some banks routinely charge fees for things like processing transactions, withdrawing money, and even transferring funds from one account to another. If your financial institution charges such fees, shop around. Competition can be fierce among financial institutions, and you can probably find one with free savings and checking accounts.

3. Find a decent interest rate. Every bank is different, so if you find more than one institution with free accounts, check the interest rates they offer. Choose the one that pays you the most for doing business with it.

Look into minimum balance requirements. Some banks charge a fee if your balance falls below the selected minimum balance. Reconsider and try to find a bank with smaller or zero balance requirements. As mentioned, it can be frustrating to withdraw money because you are facing a financial emergency and then find yourself penalized for using your own money. Shop around to find a bank that does not practice this policy.

START SMALL BUT PLAY THE LONG GAME

Committing to your financial goals does not end in a few years—it's a commitment that lasts a lifetime. It will be much easier to start by taking small steps toward your goal and adding new steps as the old ones become second nature. It's a lot like improving your running ability in basic training; you begin with one mile and slowly build up your speed and mileage as you improve over time.

Once you're comfortable with that first savings experience, consider opening multiple savings accounts. Having more than one savings account allows you to designate funds for specific goals. By designating portions of your income to specific accounts, you can track their status at a glance. It's sort of an advanced version of the old envelope savings plan.

OPEN MULTIPLE SAVINGS ACCOUNTS

The first savings account can be your emergency expense account. This money is for emergencies only such as the loss of a job, unanticipated medical expenses from an illness or injury, a death in the family, etc.

The second savings account should be for larger expenses and purchases over the long term. Examples include furniture, home maintenance and improvements, vehicle maintenance and repairs, vacations, etc.

The third savings account can be your retirement savings account. This account gives you the ability to store funds after maxing out an IRA. Because you can withdraw funds without penalty from this account, you can still apply a portion of these savings to a diversity of investments such as certificates of deposit, Roth IRAs, mutual funds, etc.

A Closer Look at the Emergency Expense Account

Before you begin paying off debts, it's vital to have at least a small emergency fund established. Without a cushion of money that can absorb unforeseen expenses, you can be financially devastated.

To begin, set an attainable goal of $1,000. You can add to it as you improve the accuracy of your budget. When you're just starting out, the ideal target amount for an emergency fund is the equivalent of three to six months' worth of living expenses. This amount should be sufficient for most expenses as they arise. You'll know if and when you need a larger emergency cushion to fall back on.

How Do You Fund Your Emergency Account?

On a budget that's already spread thin, funding your emergency account can be challenging. This might be why the average consumer doesn't have an emergency fund account. However difficult, make it a priority.

Some people treat their emergency fund as if it were a mandatory monthly bill. They pay into their emergency fund account each month as if they were paying their electric or gas bill. In this way, even if funds are withdrawn, the money is already beginning to be replaced the following month.

Other people place a large amount of money into the account all at once, sometimes from a tax return or reenlistment bonus.

However you manage it, make sure you set aside emergency funds. I cannot stress how important this is for maintaining your financial security and helping you avoid debt.

Where Should You Store Emergency Funds?

You can place your emergency funds in a money market account or a savings account. A money market account is a financial account that pays interest based on current interest rates. Typically, money market accounts have higher rates of return than traditional savings accounts, but the account limits how many withdrawals you're allowed per month. Money market accounts can also require a minimum balance, anywhere from $1,000 to $25,000 to earn interest or avoid costly fees. If a money market account is utilized as an emergency fund, these criteria aren't all bad since they deter owners from making hasty withdrawals.

Both money market accounts and savings accounts have low risk and excellent liquidity, which means it's easy to withdraw cash. I use a savings account *and* a money market account. The money market account has a slightly higher interest rate and is slightly less accessible than a savings account, which lets me withdraw cash on the spot instead of waiting a day or two. This decreases the chance I'll spend the money on nonemergency expenses.

When I have three months' worth of living expenses in my savings account, I move one month's worth of expenses into a money market account. That way, I have some emergency funds available at all times and the peace of mind that more could be available from the money market account if necessary. This technique lets me maximize the earning potential of my emergency savings, but there's no reason to make your own plan this complex. Simply saving up six months' worth of living expenses in a regular savings account is a perfect way to begin. The main idea is to consistently replenish any funds that are withdrawn and to use the money only when you face a real emergency.

Use Your Emergency Fund Only for Emergencies!

Once you've established an emergency account, you might find the money it contains extraordinarily tempting. You must remind yourself that the name of the account says it all—emergency funds. You need to develop the willpower to honestly assess what does and does not constitute an emergency.

It can also be tempting to use these designated funds to pay off existing debt. This is understandable, but if you do this and then find yourself facing an emergency, you might use credit and end up right back where you started. A better idea is to fund your emergency account and then forget it exists.

ADJUST YOUR FUNDING AS NEEDED

Implementing a savings plan can be difficult. In order to ease the pain while you're changing your spending habits, keep in mind that you can adjust your plan at any time.

For instance, suppose that after you save everything you can for three months, you find it necessary to dip into your emergency savings fund to make ends meet. If this is the case, the amount you were saving was probably a bit too much. Use only what you need in order to get by and then adjust your plan so that you are saving consistently but a little less each month. It's important to hit your goals even if you have to adjust them. Success breeds success.

On the other hand, there might be times in life when you can increase your savings such as when you receive a pay raise, promotion, tax return, or reenlistment bonus. At other times, you might need to decrease your savings such as when you have a new baby or are afflicted with an injury or illness. As life continues, you'll begin to realize your finances continually need adjusting.

KNOW THAT DIFFERENT PEOPLE HAVE DIFFERENT NEEDS

At this point, you hopefully understand why it's so beneficial to save, especially while you're young. This is true even if you don't think you need a million dollars. It's true even if you're not planning on staying in the military for 30 years. You don't have to follow the specifics outlined here in order to follow the general theme. This advice works in the civilian world too. Determine your wants and needs and how much you will need to secure your lifestyle during retirement, and then use the principles you have learned here to help you reach your goals.

PAT YOURSELF ON THE BACK

At times, it might seem like you're the only one who has ever struggled to save money, but this isn't true. Even people with the most frugal lifestyles can become overwhelmed by the difficulty of saving money. But when you realize that you don't even miss the things you are getting by without, investing your money becomes more rewarding. When your savings plan is established and the money in your accounts begins to grow more rapidly, your thrifty spending habits become easier to maintain.

By reading this book and learning how to plan for a financially sound future, you are well ahead of the game. Give your plan time to develop and mature. You will be extremely proud when it does, so take a second to pat yourself on the back. Just by reading this far, you have done more for yourself, financially, than the average person your age. Congratulations!

CHAPTER 11

THE NEXT
LEVEL OF
INVESTING

*A*ir Force Staff Sergeant Judy Levitt tells a fascinating family story. Growing up, she didn't realize that a military career could be a path to lifetime financial security. Intrigued to learn her Aunt Caroline had retired financially secure, basically set for life, after 22 years of service as a major, Staff Sergeant Levitt joined the Air Force at age 20.

Within reason, she realized her Aunt Caroline could do whatever she wanted and be assured of a comfortable lifestyle. She could try a new job and quit if she didn't like it rather than punching a clock every day to make rent. She could live in a comfortable but not huge home, drive a nice but not fancy car, and take good but not luxury vacations.

Staff Sergeant Levitt asked her Aunt Caroline, the retired major, how she had managed to put away enough of her military earnings and invest wisely enough to buy a ranch in Montana and work part-time at something she loved, breeding Tennessee Walking Horses.

Aunt Caroline explained that during basic training, she'd learned about savings bonds. She already knew that bonds typically yielded a lower return than certain other investments, but now she learned they were an extremely secure place to invest her hard-earned pay. The security of the bonds and the low risk were appealing, so once she arrived at her first duty station, she began purchasing $50 savings bonds. Throughout her enlistment, she told her niece, she continued to increase the amount of savings bonds she purchased based on the amount of increased pay she received.

Not surprisingly, Staff Sergeant Levitt decided to follow in her aunt's financial footsteps as well as her professional footsteps.

⌒

Those bonds—U.S. government savings bonds, in this case—were a simple way to lay the foundation for an investment plan for life. Of course, Aunt Caroline noted that much of her financial success was a result of developing good spending habits early in her career, especially staying away from credit cards. It took discipline, especially at the beginning, but as time went by and her pay increased, she began to see her savings increase tremendously. This became a significant motivating factor.

Most people start investing with savings accounts, but many ·ally look for alternatives, both to get a higher interest rate ᵊrsify, to spread their money among various accounts and ᭐ they don't keep all their eggs in one basket.

If you put every penny you save into your old pal's startup craft brewery and it folds after a couple of years, you're left with nothing to show. It's better to spread the risk, to hedge your bets. There's nothing wrong with putting some money in a risky investment like a business started by a friend, but make that risky investment only with money you can afford to lose after you have spread your savings over several safer accounts.

When is it the right time to move beyond the basic bank savings account or credit union savings account to the next level of investing? When should you invest in U.S. savings bonds or money market accounts or certificates of deposits (CDs) or managed investment funds? Or start buying stocks in individual companies or higher-risk startups like your buddy's craft brewery?

There's no easy answer. The time to move to the next level doesn't come after a certain number of years or a certain number of dollars. Like everything else about personal finance, it's personal. When and where you put money depends on you—your earnings, your spending, your obligations, your family, your net worth to date, and especially your hopes and desires. If you're young and relatively footloose and fancy free, you might try a risky investment even if you don't have much in savings. You can probably recover, through future earnings and savings, even if you take a loss. But if you've got young kids and have a tight budget, you probably want to hold your savings close; this money is too critical for your family's well-being to risk a loss.

This is also true if you're approaching retirement. As we get older, our investment "profile" narrows to safer investments. We can't afford to lose much because we don't have as much time and energy to earn and save more.

Ultimately, your readiness to move to the next level depends on your finances, your personality, your willingness to take risks, and how you feel. Here are some types of investments to consider when you're ready to move beyond the basic savings and checking accounts.

COMMON INVESTMENTS BEYOND BASIC SAVINGS AND CHECKING ACCOUNTS

The options for investing your money are many and varied.

Before you begin, understand your expectations so that you can decide which investment options are suitable for you. The type of investment depends on the need and time horizon you anticipate. Educate yourself as best you can and speak to a professional financial planner prior to making any monetary commitments. Keep in mind that in order to lower your risk exposure, it is wise to invest in different investment instruments and create a diversified portfolio. Start slowly, learn as you go, and be consistent about sticking with your plan.

There are countless investment opportunities and strategies available, so how do you know which are right for you? A financial planner can help, as can your banker, but even the friendliest, most affordable professionals don't understand you better than you do. It's important to be confident about moving to the next level, and that requires knowledge. The following information offers an overview of basic investments, but these definitions and descriptions are only meant to be used as a guide. Every investment is different and needs to be examined carefully before you hand over your hard-earned military pay.

Certificates of Deposit (CDs)

A CD is a promissory note from a financial institution designed as a timed deposit that restricts the holder from withdrawing funds on demand. It is a relatively low-risk instrument that yields a moderate annual percentage rate. Banks and credit unions use the money generated from CDs to fund their investments. In return, they pay interest to you since they're borrowing your money. In essence, the banks pay you one interest rate and then charge the person borrowing money from them a higher interest rate. In the end, both you and the financial institution earn a profit. Your reward for giving up the convenience of withdrawing your money whenever you like is the higher interest rate you earn compared to the rate a savings account earns, for example.

CDs are offered with various lengths of time until their maturity. Maturity dates typically range from three months to seven years. If need be, you can usually withdraw your money before the CD matures but are charged a fee for doing so. If you purchase a one-year CD for $10,000 with an interest rate of 1.8%, it would earn about $180. After one year, you would have $10,180.

Advantages of CDs include the following:
- They have a low investment risk
- They have a higher rate of return than a standard savings account
- Initial investments and interest earned are protected up to $250,000 by the FDIC
- They are short- to medium-term investments so they offer earnings sooner than long-term investments

- Typically, no fees are required to purchase CDs
- They offer peace of mind and financial security that you cannot get from stock-market-based investments

Disadvantages of CDs are as follows:

- The interest rate is locked in until the maturity date so if interest rates go up, the rate on your CD will remain the same
- CDs are subject to all applicable taxes at the local, state, and federal levels
- There can be steep penalties for withdrawing funds early
- CDs may be "callable," which means that while you cannot withdraw your money early without penalty, the financial institution can possibly call back your CD before the term ends
- Interest typically does not start accruing until the beginning of the month or quarter after you open your CD

Bonds

Although Aunt Caroline was successful with numerous investments throughout her career, she considered savings bonds to be her bread-and-butter investment and an excellent way to begin investing. "Without starting with the basics, like I did with bonds, I might not have been motivated to learn about other financial tools. Start small and you'll grow big," was the philosophy Aunt Caroline passed on to her niece, Staff Sergeant Judy Levitt.

Bonds are sold by federal, state, and local governments, public utilities companies, and other institutions in an effort to raise capital through borrowing. Basically, the issuer of the bond promises to pay your money back, with interest, on a specified maturity date. Payments received from a discount bond are paid at the date of maturity. A coupon bond pays a specific amount at the date of maturity in addition to providing a fixed payment over a specified period of time. A good example is a U.S. Treasury bond, which is probably the safest unsecured bond because of the limited risk of default by the issuer.

IRAs (Individual Retirement Accounts)

An IRA is a retirement plan that provides tax advantages. The funds placed in the IRA are not initially taxed and income earned is not taxed until it is withdrawn at retirement.

After funds have been placed in an IRA, the owner of the account advises the director of the financial institution of his or her choice of investments. An IRA owner can select from many types of investments and financial tools. Some institutions, however, limit your choices to traditional brokerage accounts such as stocks, bonds, and mutual funds.

Funds can be withdrawn at any time, but there are penalties for early withdrawal. Taxes are due for the amount withdrawn during each tax year. The exception is that funds can be withdrawn as taxable income at any time after the age of 59 and a half (this is retirement age as defined in the terms of an IRA) without penalty.

Roth IRAs

In a Roth IRA, you pay taxes on the front end on the money you invest as it is deposited into your account. Thereafter, your deposited money and interest accumulates tax free. Once you reach retirement age (again, 59 and a half), you can withdraw money from the account as an income source and withdrawals are tax free.

When you initially begin investing, you might not consider the advantages of tax strategies. Instead, you will likely be focused on making your money grow. The following example reveals the long-term tax advantage of a Roth IRA.

Let's say you establish a Roth IRA with $1,000 when you enlist in the military at age 18. You pay about 25% in taxes up front so only $750 is actually invested. By the time you retire at age 65, that $750 has the potential to grow to approximately $5,000. When you withdraw that money, you receive every penny and pay no additional taxes.

In comparison, if you had invested in a mutual fund that earned the same amount, taxes would apply to the money at the time of withdrawal. If you pay 25% of $1,000 on the front end, it's only $250. But if you pay 25% of $5,000, you're looking at $1,250, so the fund would yield only $3,750.

If you invested the maximum amount in a Roth IRA every year from the age of 18 until the age of 60, $5,500.00 per year with a 4% APR, the account balance would be about $748,000. Not too bad, eh? The best part is that every penny of that $748,000 is yours since you already paid the taxes on it years ago. Investing in a Roth IRA is one of the simplest and smartest investment moves a young person can make!

Deferred Income Plans

A deferred income plan is an investment option that allows an employee to save for retirement while deferring payment of taxes on both annual income and investment earnings on the amount placed in the fund until withdrawal. Often, larger companies will match a percentage of your contributions.

Investors choose the investments they want their deferred income funds invested into; often, stock in the company they work for is one of their options. These deferred income plans might include an employer's matching funds and are referred to by IRS tax code numbers such as 401(k), 457, and 403b.

Mutual Funds

Mutual funds pool their investors' funds into a larger fund overseen by a team of professional investment managers. This fund is then invested into a portfolio of various assets or combinations of assets. It might include investment in stocks, bonds, options, futures, currencies, treasuries, and money market securities.

The main concept of a mutual fund is diversification. Your money is spread out across many types of investments so there's a chance that if one investment is down, another is up. There is less chance of losing money in a mutual fund because diversification lessens the risk of loss.

Mutual funds vary in content and risk. Information regarding the plethora of mutual funds available can be discussed further with your financial advisor. At the time this edition was printed, there were more than 10,000 mutual funds available in North America.

No matter what type of investor you are, there is bound to be a mutual fund that fits your style.

Stocks

A stock is also known as a share or equity. Basically, a share of stock is a percentage of ownership of a company or corporation. For example, if a company issued 1,000,000 shares of stock, then 10,000 shares would represent 1% ownership. This ownership gives the owners of the stock the opportunity to benefit from a corporation's profits.

If the stock price in a company you hold goes up, you make money because your shares are now worth more. This typically happens if a company is earning profits or if speculators anticipate that a company will do well in the future. On the other hand, if a company shows a loss of profits and the share price drops, then you, as a shareholder, lose money.

Some stocks pay dividends—typically a small percentage of their value—if the company has a good year. Some high-performing companies pay dividends to their shareholders year after year, but it would be foolish to buy a stock thinking you are going to get rich off of dividends or that dividends can soften the blow if things turn bad for the company. Dividends are often paid in cash, but sometimes a company will offer dividends in additional stock for shareholders.

Index Exchange Traded Funds (ETF)

An index ETF consists of shares of stock from several companies categorized within a specific market index. This fund attempts to imitate a particular stock index of an individual financial market.

Most ETFs attempt to equal the stock market but not outperform it. In other words, the goal of an ETF is to match the returns of a specific stock index such as the S&P 500 or Dow Jones.

ETFs are not always 100% accurate when it comes to mirroring a market, but at times they have been known to outperform the markets they are attempting to mirror. If you are just beginning to invest, ETFs can be a safe and lucrative avenue.

PAY YOURSELF FIRST

In the world of personal finance and investing, "paying yourself first" has become a common phrase. Defined, it means prioritizing your investment plan over all other spending. In other words, you invest in your future before you spend or pay other expenses. You do this by routing a specified amount of money from each paycheck directly into your investment plan. Consequently, you pay yourself first.

Automatically depositing this money into your investment plan means you never see it so the money is rarely missed. This ensures that you will continue to make your chosen savings contributions month after month. This automatic approach also removes the temptation to spend investment money on other items before each monthly contribution is made.

How much should you pay yourself? There is no single answer to this question, only recommendations and guidelines. The answer is different for all of us. Some financial experts suggest that if you save 10% of your gross income, you'll have a comfortable retirement. However, this depends on numerous factors, including:

- The age of the investor
- The number of projected years until retirement

- The amount of income saved over the investor's lifetime
- Lifestyle expectations at retirement age
- Current liabilities (debt)
- Current assets (do you own your home or owe a mortgage)
- The amount of return you receive on your investments

Because service members' circumstances vary widely, the simple solution to invest 10% of your gross income might not be appropriate for you. It might be conceivable for a married couple to save 50% of their net income and still live a comfortable lifestyle. On the other hand, a new recruit just starting a career in the military might choose to start with 5%.

No matter what amount you deem appropriate, it is critical to begin today. Start developing the habits of saving and investing. Remember, these are lifelong skills you are developing, and they will change as your life changes. Your goal is to get rich slowly.

CHAPTER 12

YOU'RE SPECIAL:
MILITARY
ADVANTAGES

*T*he first time she set eyes on the young American airman sta-
tioned in her native Philippines, Charmaine knew he was the
guy for her. After their marriage, she cheerfully embarked
on several years of globetrotting as she followed her husband's postings
with the U.S. Air Force. One of their sons was born in England and the
other two in Japan. When they received orders for Davis Monthan Air
Force Base in Tucson, Arizona, they had spent very little time in the
States but were thrilled to be heading "home."

*The couple found a house pretty quickly but discovered they always
seemed to be buying something. Whether it was something for the
house, the kids, or themselves, it was always something.*

"We lived overseas for so long that we didn't have things like appliances, nor did we really understand how to shop the American way," Charmaine recalls."

Soon, the family discovered the value of smart shopping, starting with the AAFES base store. They forgot about the "public" stores and spent their money on base, especially for major purchases.

"The PX/BX and commissaries had price matching, no sales tax, and their great selection of products gave me an excellent starting point," Charmaine says. "We got a washer, dryer, refrigerator, stove, and everything else we needed with a 110 plug through the military. That shopping saved our family over $2,800 just on those basics."

Looking back, Charmaine says those bargains, and continued smart shopping, much of it thanks to base discounts, made the move go better and paved the way to good budget-based living for years to come. "Our smart shopping and first-time homebuyers credit gave us the boost to our income we needed to start our life with our military family in America," she says. "It felt great to be home without the huge cost."

～

You're special, you who serve in the military. But like Charmaine and her family, you need to take advantage of the opportunities that are uniquely available to military people. You should be aware of the shopping bargains, of course, but you should also be aware of what the military offers in terms of the Blended Retirement System (BRS) and investments. Both offer advantages and disadvantages in the long- and short-term.

One of the remarkable benefits for recruits entering the military at an early age is the immediate steady source of income. All young recruits should be aware of this distinct advantage. While many young people, even college grads, bounce from gig to gig, young people in the military have both work security and a regular paycheck. In addition to the pride you take in military service, your steady source of income is the opportunity of a lifetime. By contributing to a financial plan from the very start of your enlistment, you can position yourself for significant financial gains.

Based merely on the military pay scale, it might appear that service members do not make a lot of money, but quite the opposite is true. When considering the expenses absorbed by the benefits received, a sizable portion of a service member's income can be invested for the future.

This is due in large part to the service members' limited financial obligations. In addition to base pay, service members are typically provided with housing and food. Civilian college graduates have to provide housing and food themselves and often don't begin saving until years after earning a bachelor's degree or higher. Military recruits can begin saving the same amount of money as their civilian counterparts at a significantly earlier age. This seemingly small difference can create a tremendous difference in an investment portfolio thanks to compounding interest.

SERVICE MEMBER
VERSUS COLLEGE GRADUATE

In 2017, the average student graduating from college walked across the stage with both a diploma and $39,400 in student loan debt.

Students generally have to repay these loans through monthly install-ments that can stretch over a decade or more. The same amount of money used to repay the student loans would have enormous growth potential if placed in an investment plan instead of being used to meet the minimum monthly installments. Money that is committed to paying off student loans will never reach a graduate's savings portfolio.

Let's take a look at the investment potential of a 25-year-old successful graduate student entering the workforce for the first time and an 18-year-old private serving in the U.S. military. In the scenario represented below, both the graduate student and the 18-year-old private share a goal of retiring at the age of 60.

	Years to Age 60	Interest Rate	Monthly Investment	Initial Investment	Accumulated Savings
Student (at college graduation)	35	4%	$400.00	$0.00	$365,492.37
Recruit who does not invest enlistment bonus	42	4%	$400.00	$0.00	$522,070.40
Recruit who invests enlistment bonus	42	4%	$400.00	$20,000.00 (enlistment bonus)	$629,082.13

As you can see, if the recruit saves her $20,000 enlistment bonus, the difference is nearly a quarter of a million dollars with just seven additional years of saving.

New recruits have decades of potential accumulation and com-pounding ahead of them. It is easy to earmark a portion of your earnings to be automatically invested in a tax-advantaged retirement account. The benefit of initiating your plan as soon as you receive your first paycheck is the most important lesson in this book.

MILITARY RETIREMENT VERSUS CIVILIAN

Completing a 20- to 30-year career in the U.S. military gives service members the opportunity to design a financial plan utilizing the Blended Retirement System (BRS) that potentially surpasses that of the average civilian.

By contrast, throughout the course of their working careers, civilians often face the challenging task of maintaining retirement funds entirely on their own. Contributions from their employers might improve their bottom line, but a large portion of their savings comes out of their own pockets.

Complete with a health plan, the military's BRS is difficult to match in the private sector. For more information, contact your unit's finance department.

MONEY-SAVING ADVANTAGES OF MILITARY SERVICE

Let's take a closer look at some common advantages of serving in the military that are often overlooked.

On-Post Housing and Barracks Accommodations

Quite commonly, the largest monthly expense for a civilian is a mortgage payment or rent. By contrast, those who serve in the military are assigned to a barracks room or officer quarters, and their only responsibility is keeping it clean. Married couples are also sometimes able to live in on-post government housing. There are a number of benefits associated with living in on-post housing:

- Introduction of junior personnel into the military culture
- Promotion of military values
- A sense of community
- Support from neighbors during deployments
- Security
- Convenience (short commute or no commute at all)
- Cohesiveness with other military families

Although service members and their families consider these nontangible benefits significant, they might not regard them as the deciding factor when determining whether to live on or off post. Primarily, service members choose to live on post for economic reasons. Living on post is extremely cost-effective since individuals living in government housing have no out-of-pocket expenses for rent or utilities. This in turn allows them to earmark a generous portion of their monthly income toward long-term investments.

Basic Allowance for Housing (BAH)

Qualified military members who choose to reside off post receive a monthly housing allowance known as basic allowance for housing, or BAH. This is a monthly flat rate issued to qualified service members. In general, the amount depends on location, rank, and number of dependents. Recipients of the BAH who spend less on housing than the amount they receive do not have their allowance reduced. These remaining funds can potentially be invested. For further information regarding eligibility and the use of BAH, make an appointment at your unit's finance and housing departments.

Health Insurance

Civilians who retire early do not qualify for government health care such as Medicare. These civilians must purchase health coverage with money taken from their retirement plans. The cost can be extremely high and depends on factors such as age and potential health problems. By contrast, individuals retiring from the military have full medical coverage. This is a remarkable financial benefit that gives service members valuable peace of mind.

Post-9/11 GI Bill

On June 22, 1944, President Franklin Delano Roosevelt signed into law the Servicemen's Readjustment Act of 1944, commonly known as the GI Bill of Rights. The GI Bill is an education benefit earned through active duty, selected reserve, and National Guard service. The benefit is designed to assist service members and eligible veterans with the cost of getting an education or formal training.

The GI Bill was revamped in 1984 by former Mississippi Congressman Gillespie V. "Sonny" Montgomery and became known as the "Montgomery GI Bill."

Most recently, in 2008, the GI Bill was updated and enacted into law by Congress and is currently referred to as the Post-9/11 GI Bill. This bill is possibly the most significant piece of legislation pertaining to service members ever produced by the United States government. For additional information regarding the Post-9/11 GI Bill and educational benefits you might be eligible to receive, contact your unit's finance department.

PX/BX

Another military cost-saving advantage is shopping at the military exchange services, also known as the Post Exchange (PX) and Base Exchange (BX). The exchange can provide outstanding values that are only available to military personnel. Savings on groceries, electronics, and clothing can add up fast, and money saved can go directly into a retirement savings plan.

Short Work Commute

Living on base often allows military personnel to walk to work. Compare this to the cost of the average daily commute for most civilians. If you think the amount of money involved is negligible, think again.

A 30-minute commute from the suburbs to a large city can easily be 25 miles. If gasoline costs $3.85 a gallon, a daily 50-mile commute in a vehicle that gets 25 miles to the gallon can cost $100.00 or more each month, not counting the vehicle's maintenance costs, insurance, and wear and tear or depreciation.

Comparatively, service members who live on base pay next to nothing, and the money they save can be directed into their investment plans.

Thrift Savings Plan (TSP)

Typically, the thrift savings plan is the simplest way to begin investing. Sponsored by the federal government, this retirement and savings plan provides retirement income to service members. The fees involved are minuscule compared to other investment firms, making the TSP an excellent tool to begin your investment strategy. For more information, visit your unit's finance department.

Thrift Savings Plan Life Cycle Fund (TSP "L" Fund)

Thrift Savings Plans now offer "Life Cycle Funds" to those interested in saving for retirement. A Life Cycle Fund diversifies your investments based on your target retirement date. The farther away the determined date, the more risk that can be taken, and vice versa. As you get closer to your target retirement date, your Life Cycle Fund investments become more conservative while still providing the highest possible rate of return. The best part about the TSP Life Cycle Fund is that you do not need to make any of these difficult decisions yourself. Decisions are made by professional fund managers whose only job is to make the most of your money based on your age and projected date of retirement. The TSP "L" Fund is an excellent tool to begin your investment strategy. For more information, visit your unit's finance department.

Savings Deposit Program (SDP)

The military's Savings Deposit Program was first established during the Vietnam era. In 2018, the SDP enabled service members serving in designated combat zones to earn 10% interest per year on a maximum investment of $10,000. Interest stops accruing 90 days after you leave the combat zone. The SDP is an excellent guaranteed investment opportunity that allows all deployed service members to earn a fixed interest rate higher than any other comparable investment. As always, for more information, visit your unit's finance department.

TIME IS MONEY

From a young person's perspective, the statement "I have plenty of time; I'll start saving later" might appear compelling. However, after investigating the arithmetic, it's obvious why taking advantage of the time you have on your side early in your military career is a better option. But if you still think you can make up for the time that's slipping away, look at the example in the table below, which illustrates the benefit of investing as much as you can as early as you can.

Age of Investor	Years to Retiring at Age 65	APR	Initial Investment	Monthly Deposit	Amount of Savings
45	20	5%	$0.00	$450.00	$184,965.15
35	30	5%	$0.00	$450.00	$374,516.39
25	40	5%	$0.00	$450.00	$686,709.07
18	47	5%	$0.00	$450.00	$1,018,926.11

As you can see, time literally *is* money! Take advantage of the special advantages available only to you, a member of the military, to invest wisely and save.

CHAPTER 13

DEPLOYMENT
FINANCES

*M*ajor Thomas Magee learned irreplaceable financial lessons over his 28-plus years as an Army Reserve officer, especially during and after his deployments to Iraq and Afghanistan.

"The public doesn't realize what a war or a long deployment does both to your financial mind and to your bank account," he says. "Deployments can help the bank account for sure. You get extra pay when you deploy, but the really big benefit to the checkbook comes not from more money but from less time to spend it. It's like you're locked up in the wilderness—no place to spend money and nothing to spend it on."

Through the wonders of direct deposit, those deployment paychecks fatten up the back account. More in, almost nothing out.

"So when you come home, you feel like you've hit the lottery," Magee says. He elaborates, "Returning soldiers are confronted with some very difficult issues. You come back to civilian life with this built-up, overpowering desire for a brand new vehicle, new clothes, electronics, boats, all-terrain vehicles, and everything else that can potentially drain your bank account. You want to go out immediately to make up for lost time. You're tempted to purchase the new things you've always wanted but couldn't afford. Any reasoning by others, or from your conscience, to moderate your spending is overlooked by the excuse that you deserve to make the purchase because you were away on a long deployment."

In his first war, Desert Storm, Magee worked at a POW camp as a first lieutenant, helping oversee prisoners of war in the Saudi Arabian desert. When he came home, he admits that he "lived it up." Before he knew it, all that built-up cash was gone.

Sixteen years later, he went to war again, this time as a major advising the Iraqi Army. When he came home, he was pleased to see that his bank account was considerably larger than the first time he'd deployed. He vowed not to repeat the same mistakes. This windfall of money was an opportunity to make a long-range, lifelong change.

"I made up my mind back in the desert of Iraq," Major Magee explains. "I wasn't going to make the same mistake I did after Desert Storm. I wanted to get something for my sacrifice. I set goals to help me in numerous ways."

Magee's ultimate goal, he explained, was to buy his first home.

$\sim$

Since September 11, 2001, the potential for deployment while serving in the United States military has increased significantly. For peace of mind, it's best to thoroughly prepare your financial plan before you're notified that you're going overseas. Then, if a deployment is announced, you can simply put your preorganized plan into motion. Preparing how to handle your money before, during, and after each phase of deployment requires careful attention.

Although a deployment certainly includes health and safety risks, the financial benefits can definitely be viewed in a positive light. Taking advantage of well-defined financial opportunities available during a deployment can result in financial security for you and your family. Why waste such a unique opportunity by frivolously spending the additional money on luxury items that have little or no long-term value? Cashing in on the additional income you receive while deployed can provide a hefty boost to your investment portfolio.

PREPARE FOR DEPLOYMENT

To state the obvious, preparing for a military deployment can be extremely stressful for service members and their families. Being separated from family and experiencing other lifestyle changes can at times be overwhelming.

One of the biggest stressors is organizing and maintaining finances. Even while traveling halfway around the world, you're still responsible for the financial obligations you leave behind. If you're unable to track your spending, you might accumulate an untold amount of financial debt that will be waiting for you upon your return. If you don't prepare for your monetary commitments ahead of time, you can find yourself dealing with adverse consequences up to and including bankruptcy.

However, constructing a solid financial plan well in advance will alleviate one of the leading causes of anxiety while deployed. Organizing your finances will give you a sense of empowerment, and a robust savings account will certainly provide something to look forward to when you get back home. You'll literally turn the number one stressor into a positive goal.

Because a deployment can drastically change your finances, it's important to construct or reconstruct your financial plan to reflect the time you'll be away. If you're married, it's imperative that you design your plan with your spouse. As mentioned, struggling with finances is one of the most common problems military families experience during deployment. Getting organized well in advance and working as a team allows couples to minimize confusion and avoid costly miscommunications. Consider implementing the following tips before you deploy.

Adjust Your Current Budget

Prepare your finances to reflect your anticipated change in income and expenses for the designated period of time you'll be away. Begin by reviewing your current monthly household expenses and then adding or subtracting any differences for the time you expect to be deployed. This adjusted budget should give you a good idea of what financial issues you and your family will face each month. As a bonus, it might also reveal ways you can save money during deployment. Moreover, the adjusted budget will provide critical information to whomever you designate to handle your finances while you're gone. By providing an accurate and detailed plan, you can rest assured you've minimized the possibility of coming home to financial discrepancies and chaos.

Open Two Checking Accounts (for Couples)

To eliminate miscommunication between spouses and avoid the possibility of overdrawing a shared checking account, many couples find it helpful to maintain two checking accounts, one for monthly household expenses and the other strictly for the deployed service member. This technique reduces the possibility of miscalculations as a result of two people half a world apart attempting to pay their expenditures from a single checking account. Just remember to be cautious not to overspend while deployed overseas.

Plan in Advance to Pay Your Bills on Time

You should make it a priority to find a way to meet all anticipated financial obligations throughout your deployment. Major expenses you might need to plan for include credit cards, automobile loans, and mortgage or rent payments. Making arrangements well in advance is your personal responsibility to yourself and your family. Doing so will give you a sense of confidence and peace of mind, and you'll be more capable of focusing on the task at hand while serving in hazardous situations.

Pay Your Bills Electronically

As mentioned earlier, many monthly bills can now be paid automatically through an electronic process by your financial institution. This is extremely convenient when you're on deployment.

This process works especially well for bills that don't fluctuate such as automobile notes and mortgages. Contact your financial institution and ask to be advised of any available options. Automatic bill pay is:

- Easy to set up
- Eliminates a significant responsibility each month
- Ensures payments will never be late or get lost
- Saves money on stamps

Request Electronic Financial Statements

Prior to deployment, I requested that my financial provider send all monthly financial statements and notifications to me via email. This allowed me to stay up to date on all account information even when I was on the other side of the world. The system works so efficiently that I still use it today. Requesting electronic financial statements:

- Allows you to receive information faster
- Eliminates lost paper documentation
- Allows you to address discrepancies before they escalate
- Eliminates surprises upon returning home
- Allows spouses to receive and access identical information
- Allows you to receive information via email or online 24/7

Pay All Bills on the Same Date

When all your bills are due on the same date, you can pay them all at once and not think about doing so again until next month. Setting this up can be as simple as contacting the billing department and requesting that the due date be changed to the date you prefer. Some people prefer to have all bills due at the beginning of the month, and some prefer the middle. There is no right or wrong way. The concept simply promotes additional organization by enforcing a consistent routine every month.

Pay Your Bills Online

If you haven't chosen to set up electronic auto bill pay, paying your bills online might be an option. Many businesses and utility companies encourage this practice. A few examples of bills you can routinely pay online include utilities, mortgage, cell phone, and auto loans.

Request a Trustworthy Person to Oversee Your Finances

Although you might set up the majority of your financial transactions to be performed electronically, you'll still probably need someone to act on your behalf while you're away. After selecting a family member or friend to fill this role, present this person with a copy of your budget and any specific instructions. Many situations will require the designee to provide proof that you've given this authority to him or her before transactions can be completed.

Appoint a Power of Attorney

Prior to deployment, it's important to appoint someone to be your power of attorney so that they can act in your place should financial or legal matters arise while you're deployed. Legally, you must provide certified documentation proving you've given someone power of attorney.

When you grant a person power of attorney, you become the grantor, and the person with this power (your agent) is authorized, or granted, the power to act on your behalf in legal or business matters. Most often, service members choose to grant power of attorney to a spouse or other trusted family member, but it's important to periodically review the designation and what it covers. Your changing needs may necessitate a revision, ensuring that your power of attorney designation accomplishes exactly what you need done and nothing else.

To establish a power of attorney, speak to your chain of command or your unit's Judge Advocate General legal department (JAG). Power of attorney is a legal instrument that deserves your serious consideration.

Consider Storage Instead of Maintaining an Apartment

If you live in an apartment when you learn you're going to be deployed, you might consider breaking your lease and putting everything into storage if losing your deposit is less expensive than paying rent for an empty apartment. This will also eliminate monthly utility expenses and potential maintenance concerns or tragedies like broken water pipes, fires, etc.

Make a Plan to Pay Income Taxes

While away on deployment, you are still responsible for paying your taxes on time. If you're unable to set this up before you deploy, you must file for an extension with the IRS. Although the forms to do so can be found online, I highly recommend that you speak with a representative of the IRS to be sure you take care of the matter properly. Decide in advance with your power of attorney how your income tax return will be filed and who will do it.

Consider a Debit Card versus a Credit Card

The difference between a credit card and a debit card is that a credit card company extends credit to you and you repay the money, with interest, for any purchases you make with the card. A debit card simply allows you to access funds directly from your checking or savings account. Since the debit card isn't a line of credit, you don't pay interest on any of your purchases. Debit cards can be used as a form of payment throughout much of the world today, making them very convenient while deployed.

Establish a Will and Consider Life Insurance

As you are well aware, military deployments involve a certain degree of risk, and it's important to consider who you want your assets to go to if you die. A will is a legal document that instructs others how you want your property distributed after your death. In addition, the military, like private corporations, offers life insurance plans. A key part of life insurance is naming a beneficiary, someone who receives the life insurance payment if you die. If you have any questions regarding either your will or your life insurance, speak to your chain of command to be directed to a professional who can ensure that you are making informed decisions. If you need further assistance, you can also visit your base's Judge Advocate General legal office (JAG).

Consider Traumatic Injury Insurance

Prior to deployment, it might be in your best interests to determine if you qualify for traumatic injury insurance. This type of protection may be offered by the Service Members' Group Life Insurance (SGLI) program.

SUMMARY OF PREDEPLOYMENT TIPS

Additional information can be provided by those within your chain of command's finance department, but some of the finer points to address before you deploy are these:

- Select a family member or friend you trust to be given power of attorney and file any appropriate paperwork
- Set up automatic bill payment whenever possible
- Select a family member you trust to take care of your bills; this person might be the same one who holds power of attorney
- Notify your current financial institutions and creditors of your deployment and provide them with contact information for your power of attorney
- Provide pertinent account numbers, user names, and passwords to your power of attorney

- Design a system to save all receipts as well as legal and financial documentation; this could be as simple as making a folder for each of these categories
- Review your life insurance policies with your providers and beneficiaries
- If at all possible, be sure you have an emergency savings account containing six months' worth of living expenses
- Take advantage of the Savings Deposit Program (SDP) while you are serving in a combat zone
- Research a traumatic injury protection policy; such policies are designed to help your family if you suffer a traumatic injury
- Complete a will and consider purchasing life insurance and traumatic injury insurance

PREDEPLOYMENT CHECKLISTS

The following checklists will help you prepare to deploy financially, legally, and in terms of your documentation.

To be sure you're financially prepared to deploy:
- Adjust your current budget to reflect your new income and expenses
- Discuss the plan thoroughly with your spouse
- Designate someone to pay the bills
- Establish two checking accounts if you're married
- Develop a plan for paying income taxes

- Consider the following in your budget:
  - ✓ Utilities
  - ✓ Rent/mortgage
  - ✓ Food
  - ✓ Auto maintenance
  - ✓ Insurance
  - ✓ Loan payments
  - ✓ Emergencies
  - ✓ Babysitting
  - ✓ Presents
  - ✓ Savings
  - ✓ Long-distance phone calls
  - ✓ Postage
  - ✓ Travel (leave)
  - ✓ Entertainment

To be sure you're legally prepared to deploy:

- Make sure your spouse's emergency contact information is on record and current
- Establish a plan for moving your household goods
- Make sure you know your spouse's Social Security number
- Designate a power of attorney
- Make sure your spouse has a government identification card
- Make sure your will is established and current

Check to be sure the following documents are up to date, in order, and secure:

- Power of attorney
- Birth certificates
- Wills
- Citizenship documentation
- Savings bonds
- Naturalization papers
- Charge account numbers
- Inventory of household goods
- Real estate (deeds, titles, mortgages, leases)
- Family Social Security numbers
- Car titles
- Bank account numbers
- Insurance policies
- Marriage certificate

DURING DEPLOYMENT

Once you are deployed, consider implementing the following ideas.

Save Your Hard-Earned Deployment Cash

From a monetary standpoint, a deployment can be the opportunity of a lifetime.

Deployment money has the potential to catapult your savings account balance well beyond your expectations. Make sure you put an investment strategy into effect *before* you leave, then watch your savings increase by leaps and bounds.

Watch Out for Temptations while Away from Home

Long deployments can increase the temptation to give in to major impulse purchases. Some bases even offer service members the opportunity to order new customized vehicles or motorcycles directly from the manufacturer. Just remember to ask yourself if these luxury items are included in your financial plan.

Avoid the "I Might Not Live to See Tomorrow" Philosophy

Those who embrace this philosophy believe, "I might as well spend it today because I might not live to see tomorrow." I watched a few soldiers in my company blow their hard-earned pay based on this philosophy before and during deployment. Guess what? They returned home broke and were right back where they started, with little to show for their 16 months in combat. Others who did not handle their finances with this attitude were in much better shape upon their return. Try establishing lofty goals such as purchasing a new home upon your return, attending college, or attaining the peace of mind that you're getting a tremendous jump start on your retirement.

Be Cautious about Borrowing Money

Be conservative and careful about taking on a loan during deployment. Base your monthly income on your post-deployment paycheck, not your deployment income.

AFTER DEPLOYMENT

With deployments spanning 12 months or more, many service members see their savings accounts increase dramatically. However, upon your return, you must adjust your spending to reflect your current pay rate at that time. Remind yourself that your monthly income could be reduced by half.

Veterans returning from deployment often purchase large-scale items as a reward for their hard work overseas. Examples could be a new vehicle, boat, ATV, snowmobile, or an extravagant wedding ceremony. The table below examines the cost of purchasing a brand new SUV compared to placing the same money in a moderate-risk mutual fund for the next 50 years.

	Funds Spent	Interest Earned	Today's Value	Value in 5 Years	Value in 50 Years
SUV	$40,000	0%	$40,000	$10,000	$0
Mutual Fund	$40,000	4%	$40,000	$48,666	$284,267

To summarize, when a deployment is announced, financial opportunities might be your last concern, but ignoring money matters at this time could be costly. The better you prepare today, the better you'll be able to protect your family and finances while you're away. For more information, an appointment with your unit's finance department will be able to provide additional assistance regarding your unique personal finance issues and specific information pertaining to your unit's anticipated deployment.

MAJOR MAGEE TODAY

Remember Major Magee? During his second deployment and after his return, he avoided the financial mistakes he made after Desert Storm. He did a lot of the things advised in this chapter, starting with stepping up his savings while overseas and becoming a smart shopper when he returned. Magee kept saving and stuck to his budget, which allowed him to fulfill his ultimate goal of purchasing a new home after his return.

CHAPTER 14

PROFESSIONAL
ADVICE AND
BUILDING WEALTH

"*J*ust *be sure to shop around before you hire a financial advisor,*" *USMC Gunnery Sergeant Lyle clearly stated.*

His first experience with a civilian financial advisor wasn't a pleasant one. After taking advantage of the military's blended retirement system (BRS), which he spoke highly of, Gunnery Sergeant Lyle had decided to invest additional funds into his retirement plan using a personal financial planner.

He explained, "Early in my career with the Corp, I was single, and it was my intention to salt away extra funds I accumulated through re-enlistment bonuses, tax returns, and whatnot. When I was young,

I figured all investment companies were the same, so I funded an account with the first company I found. After a few interactions, I felt as though the advisor was speaking down to me. He used technical terms I didn't understand, and he didn't take the time to explain them. More than that, it was completely unclear how the company charged fees and commissions. Different investment opportunities the advisor promoted seemed unsuitable to my long-term goals, and when the advisor pushed the sale, I felt he didn't have my best interests at heart. After determining that the company was putting its interests before mine, it was time to leave. I closed the account, and, yes, there was a penalty for that too!

"However, I didn't want to give up. I had long-term goals, and I considered the mistake of not examining this company prior to hiring it a learning experience. After researching several additional investment companies and learning exactly how each charged fees and commissions, I decided to give investing a second chance, and I opened an account with a new financial planner. Coincidently, the company I chose specialized in serving the U.S. military. As of today, I've used the company's services for more than a decade, and my portfolio has grown well beyond my expectations.

"As a final word, be sure to scrutinize the companies you're considering. Although you hire a financial planner for the broader, deeper investing knowledge you don't have, you won't have anything if you don't have a relationship based on trust."

⁓

When it comes to personal finance, there's always more to learn. Talk to people and attend free lectures and workshops, but don't be eager to sign on with any individual financial advisor or company.

Likewise, don't just automatically follow any one piece of advice. Question everyone and everything to determine whether the advice is right for you and your situation right now. Look at other advice, at other strategies. Is it a good strategy but not right for you at this stage? Review the process described earlier for figuring out your spending profile and what type of advisor you need. Go back to what you've learned about your long-range goals and your saving and investing preferences. Then you can figure out who you might want to work with and determine how to find that person.

You naturally want to work with someone you like and are comfortable with, someone who is positive and inspires confidence, someone you trust. Of those qualities, trust is the most important. Think about it. Who would you rather have as a financial advisor? Someone you like a lot who always paints a rosy picture of every investment, every financial move, or someone a little brusque and crusty who might seem overly pessimistic and cautious but who has a better track record of returning good results and making money for his or her clients? Case closed.

Dealing with professional advisors is typically part of the bigger picture in terms of long-range asset management. Long-range asset management is code, or cocktail party talk, for "getting rich." Bigger picture topics involve how your investment profile might change as you acquire a home, insurance, and other assets. This long-range planning also involves estate planning, managing taxes, and the generational transfer of wealth to your kids. It involves gifts you can give that work for you as long as you're still alive. It involves the potential importance of managing your tax exposure. It also involves tips for planning and managing your retirement:

how and when you will know you have enough, and how well you can live when you stop working.

INVESTING OVERVIEW

At this point, you have a grasp on the concept that investing your money is really a series of steps that you take. You've learned that it's a good idea to have the following in place before entering into an advanced financial plan:

- A comprehensive list of short- and long-term goals
- An established budget
- A savings account
- A checking account
- A fully funded emergency account (the equivalent of six months' worth of living expenses)
- All debt eliminated (except a mortgage)

Once you've accomplished these basics, you have a solid foundation from which to build wealth. After you've put these critical building blocks in place, you'll be able to advance your portfolio into a broader investment plan.

WHY USE A FINANCIAL PLANNER?

Assessing an individual company's value is a time-consuming process that requires exhaustive research of numerous facets and financial documentation before you can make an educated decision. But you're in luck—institutional investors called financial planners can do the work for you. Financial investment companies hire teams of professional investors to work together to analyze specific industries and companies. Together, these teams have the resources, experience, and expertise to grade a company's strengths and weaknesses.

A financial planner is a licensed professional trained to assist investors by designing financial strategies that best fit their needs. They are educated in their field and have the ability to create a detailed plan. Your planner will help you devise specific goals. He or she will work closely with you to develop a plan tailored to your needs and based on your tolerance of risk as well as your chosen timeline.

Accomplishing on your own what financial planners can do for you would be an extraordinary feat, especially if you're a beginning investor. Using a professional financial planner involves fees, but these are minuscule compared to the money you could potentially lose and the time and resources required for you to successfully manage your investments on your own.

If you do try to invest on your own, it's likely you'll learn the perils of the stock market by trial and error. More often than not, this method of learning results in the loss of the most precious commodity an investor has—time. Typical errors made by novice investors include:

- Buying and selling stocks too frequently
- Buying and selling stocks based on media that presents misleading information or misinterpreted news stories
- Basing investments on emotions like fear and greed rather than facts and substantiated information

- Selling valuable stocks too early, resulting in missed profit opportunities
- Holding declining stocks too long, deepening losses

The ability to accurately analyze an individual company's strength takes years of formal education and experience. When you are ready to begin investing, try using a qualified financial planner. The costs are well worth the return.

HOW SOON SHOULD YOU SEEK A FINANCIAL PLANNER?

It's wise to wait to invest until you've funded an emergency account and paid down any outstanding debt, but contacting a financial advisor sooner to help with decisions along the way isn't a bad idea. An advisor can provide insight that helps you accomplish your goals more efficiently. As long as you're accumulating cash in your savings account, you're saving money and earning interest, so don't feel obligated to make hasty decisions. An excellent resource to begin with is your unit's finance department.

HOW TO CHOOSE A FINANCIAL PLANNER

Be sure to write down every question you have and interview several financial planners before making your selection. Advise the planner that you're just getting started with your investment plan and that you're interested in learning as much as you can. If a planner is impatient or unwilling to answer your questions, request a different planner or choose another company. There are plenty available. Remember, your planner works for you, and he or she should value your time.

HOW DOES A FINANCIAL PLANNER GET PAID?

This is an important question. Some financial planners charge a flat fee and some charge a commission. It might be in your best interests to hire a fee-only planner as opposed to one who earns a commission. Advisors who are paid a flat fee do not have an incentive to sell you products or services you might not need.

BENEFITS OF WORKING WITH A FINANCIAL PLANNER

A professional financial planner can potentially:

- Increase your knowledge of the investment industry by answering questions you have about the process
- Provide insight during periods of market instability and notify you when an adjustment to your portfolio might be in order
- Utilize numerous resources to organize a strategy that will best meet your needs
- Advise you as to which investment opportunities are in your best interests
- Assist you in weighing risks and making decisions

THE FINAL DECISION

Do not select a financial planner until he or she has disclosed a complete guideline of all fees, penalties, and commissions you will be charged. It's imperative that you have a full understanding of how the investment company gets paid before you decide to invest.

It's easy to feel pressured or become overly excited and make hasty decisions. If you feel rushed when speaking with an investment company representative, explain that you need time to think about your decision. While you decide, your money will be safe in a savings account. Take all the time you need to make investment decisions.

BECOME A SAVVY INVESTOR

The lessons in this book focus on the importance of long-term financial planning and investing. Your financial plan will require time before it begins to turn a profit. This requires patience.

Your ability to focus on the goals that will be important to you in the future as well as the ones that are important to you right now will help you avoid impulsive spending and is critical to your success. This requires foresight.

The more you are willing to learn regarding investments and investing strategies, the greater your ability to continuously make sound decisions. Be willing to educate yourself.

Savvy investors share these basic qualities of patience, foresight, and a willingness to educate themselves. If you don't possess these qualities, do your best to develop them.

FOLLOW YOUR GUT

Given the many variables involved in sound investing, even a single conversation with a financial advisor can be helpful, but attending a workshop or talking to an advisor—even if you read a book meant to be as comprehensive and helpful as this one—does not mean you should blindly follow the advice you are given. You know yourself and what's right for you better than anyone. If it doesn't feel right at the start, it's never going to feel right. And if it seems to be too good to be true, it probably is.

DON'T FAIL
TO PLAN!

I n the immortal words of Winston Churchill, "He who fails to plan is planning to fail."

If you look back at the information in this book five, 10, even 50 years from now, will you be in debt, with no savings plan, and wondering what you were thinking when you didn't take advantage of this knowledge? Or will you feel confident and proud of yourself for securing your own financial future?

I hope it's the latter. If you feel the same way, set yourself up for financial security by following the six steps below.

1. Follow your written budget to ensure a lifestyle within your means.

2. Establish a short-term emergency fund ($2,000).

3. Establish a long-term emergency fund (six months' worth of salary).

4. Pay off your debts (including your vehicle but excluding your mortgage).

5. Interact with your financial planner and invest 15% to 25% (or more) of your income.

6. Use any excess funds (reenlistment bonuses, tax returns, and so on) to pay off your home mortgage early.

That's it. If you follow these six basic steps, the finer points will fall into place.

EDUCATE YOUR FELLOW SERVICE MEMBERS

Many new recruits have just finished high school, and the military might very well be their first steady paying job. It is highly possible that these young service members might not yet know how to set a budget or plan for their future. Without financial guidance, they might slip through the cracks and find themselves losing the most precious commodity available to them—time.

By reading this book, you've learned just how much of your financial future is within your control. Share this information with as many service members as possible and avoid learning about life's financial pitfalls through trial and error. In turn, with annual revisions and contributions from readers like you, it is my personal goal to perfect *Basic Training for Personal Military Finance* in the hopes that readers will pass on these valuable lessons to their fellow service members.

In the meantime, good luck with your military career *and* with attaining financial prosperity!

MICHAEL STEPHEN HAMLIN

E arning a degree in finance prior to enlisting in the U.S. Army as an infantryman allowed Mike Hamlin to recognize financial opportunities overlooked by his fellow soldiers. In an effort to promote awareness of the military's true earning potential, Hamlin created this invaluable money guide, a one-of-a-kind educational resource, that can change lives and manifest brilliant financial futures for all members serving in the U.S. military.